ANNIHILATE FEAR

ANNIHILATE FEAR: PEACE AND POWER FOR EVERY AREA OF YOUR LIFE

ISBN: 978-0-9988739-1-6 (English paper)
ISBN: 978-0-9988739-2-3 (English e-book)
ISBN: 978-0-9988739-3-0 (Spanish paper)
ISBN: 978-0-9988739-4-7 (Spanish e-book)

Copyright © 2021 Joan Hunter

Published by Hunter Books, an imprint of Joan Hunter Ministries
PO Box 411, Pinehurst, TX 77362 USA | JoanHunter.org, JoanHunter.ca

No part of this book may be reproduced, stored in a retrieval system or transmitted in any form or by any means – electronic, mechanical, photocopy, recording or any other – except for brief quotations, without permission in writing from the publisher.

All Scripture quotations, unless otherwise indicated, are taken from the New King James Version®. Copyright © 1982 by Thomas Nelson. Used by permission. All rights reserved. Scripture quotations marked ESV are from the ESV® Bible (The Holy Bible, English Standard Version®), copyright © 2001 by Crossway, a publishing ministry of Good News Publishers. Used by permission. All rights reserved. Scripture quotations marked MSG are taken from THE MESSAGE, copyright © 1993, 2002, 2018 by Eugene H. Peterson. Used by permission of NavPress. All rights reserved. Represented by Tyndale House Publishers, a Division of Tyndale House Ministries. Scripture quotations marked NLT are taken from the Holy Bible, New Living Translation, copyright ©1996, 2004, 2015 by Tyndale House Foundation. Used by permission of Tyndale House Publishers, a Division of Tyndale House Ministries, Carol Stream, Illinois 60188. All rights reserved. Scripture quotations marked KJV are taken from the King James Version of the Bible. Public domain. Scripture quotations marked TPT are from The Passion Translation®. Copyright © 2017, 2018 by Passion & Fire Ministries, Inc. Used by permission. All rights reserved. ThePassionTranslation.com. Scripture quotations marked AMP are taken from the Amplified® Bible (AMP), Copyright © 2015 by The Lockman Foundation. Used by permission. www.lockman.org. Scripture quotations marked TLB are taken from The Living Bible copyright © 1971. Used by permission of Tyndale House Publishers, Carol Stream, Illinois 60188. All rights reserved. Scripture quotations marked RSV are from Revised Standard Version of the Bible, copyright © 1946, 1952, and 1971 National Council of the Churches of Christ in the United States of America. Used by permission. All rights reserved worldwide.

Cover design by Yvonne Parks at PearCreative.ca
Interior typesetting by David Sluka

Printed in the United States of America
21 22 23 24 25   5 4 3 2 1

CONTENTS

1. Fear … Faith … Love 1
2. God Is for Me! 3
3. Devil, You Can't Steal My Peace! 35
4. Freedom from Fear 51
5. Fear to Faith 67
6. Develop Your Faith 79
7. What Does Love Have to Do With It? 107
   Afterword 115
   Scriptures 117
   Prayers 133
   Acknowledgements 155
   About the Author 156

1
FEAR ... FAITH ... LOVE

What is the relationship between these three powerful words? Some say faith is the opposite of fear. Others say love is the opposite of fear. Does that mean faith and love are the same thing?

We are going to consider the relationships between these three words and how they affect our lives. Is one more powerful than the other? Does each or all of them appear in our lives regardless of our actions, or do we have a choice?

The answers to these questions may not be easy, but what you choose to do may have a great influence on what you do next.

The church's definitions may not match the world's definitions either. Before going any further, I would like you to jot down what you believe about fear, faith, and love. I'm not asking you to look up the words in a dictionary or on your phone. Just jot down in a few words or sentences what you believe from your own personal experiences.

When you finish this book, I will again ask you to do the same exercise. It will be interesting to see the change(s) in what you believe.

Contrary to what some people say, there are both good and

ANNIHILATE FEAR

bad aspects to each area we will consider in this book. For example, when is fear bad? Is it ever considered to be good? Can love be bad? Or is it always good? Does faith affect fear or love? How? When?

2
GOD IS FOR ME!

Fear is a lethal weapon the devil uses to steal, kill, and destroy the Christian. The trouble with fear is that it's like smallpox or the measles. Normally, you don't have just one little spot. Just like disease symptoms come in a cluster, so does fear. You get one fear, then another, and another, and another, and another.

Almost all of us have been gripped by fear at some point in our lives. Basic fear can be healthy because it warns us of possible danger. However, it should dissipate or fade away. The spirit of fear may attack us and attempt to stay as a permanent resident. Let me tell you, fear doesn't have to stay, Don't lay out the welcome mat and allow it to take residence within you.

My parents, Charles and Frances Hunter, were in a big DC-10 airplane on their way to Canada for a ministry meeting. The plane had just taken off from the Houston airport when the plane apparently got caught in the tail end of a tornado. The plane tilted at such an angle, they wondered if the plane was going to crash right into the ground. For a moment, they felt real fear.

Fear was rapidly taking over the entire plane. Suitcases went flying through the air. Mom's purse flew up, hit the ceiling of the plane, and bounced back down onto her head. Everything that wasn't tied down was sailing around the interior of the plane.

They both freely admitted that fear gripped them ... for a moment. What did they do? Their first reaction was to immediately pray in the Spirit! What happened? The fear instantly left. Why? Because they trusted God. The moment they began praying, fear disappeared.

Fear and trust cannot exist at the same time. Praying in tongues was instantaneous because they didn't think about how or what to pray, their spirits just took over. They prayed in an unknown tongue, and God heard and answered.

Webster's Dictionary says that fear is "an unpleasant emotion caused by the belief that someone or something is dangerous, likely to cause pain, or a threat." Other words you may hear include terror, fright, fearfulness, horror, alarm, panic, agitation, trepidation, dread. You get the idea. Fear is not good or healthy. Recognize what it is and pray against those negative emotions or feelings.

As soon as Mom and Dad realized what was happening, they turned to their Father. Their trust was in Him, and fear couldn't stay.

Perhaps you are experiencing some of the most common fears, such as death, aging, sickness, failure, poverty, losing a mate, or rejection. The list could be endless. If you have any of these fears, get ready to get rid of them right now.

> There is no fear in love; but perfect love casteth out fear: because fear hath torment. He that feareth is not made perfect in love. (1 John 4:18 KJV)

> Love never brings fear, for fear is always related to punishment. But love's perfection drives the fear

> of punishment far from our hearts. Whoever walks constantly afraid of punishment has not reached love's perfection. (1 John 4:18 TPT)

The spirit of fear, a tool of the devil, causes physical suffering and mental distress. It also brings terror, panic, and horror. When fear grips you, you cannot think clearly or rationally. In fact, you may not be able to think at all.

Is there an answer to such devastating fear? What is it? Is there an antidote? There certainly is. When faith looks at a situation, fear disappears. Perfect love also destroys fear. God's Word has the answer to this kind of fear.

> So then faith comes by hearing, and hearing by the word of God! (Romans 10:17)

> Faith, then, is birthed in a heart that responds to God's anointed utterance of the Anointed One. (Romans 10:17 TPT)

The Scriptures also talk about a kind of fear that is good—the fear, or reverence, of God. The fear that brings torment does not belong in the Christian's life because God has given us the answer. We need to know and understand who we are in Christ in order to have peace in our lives. This knowledge, firmly embedded in our hearts, can dispel all the fear the devil tries to throw our way.

> For God hath not given us the spirit of fear;
> but of power, and of love, and of a sound mind.
> (2 Timothy 1:7 KJV)

BATTLING UNHEALTHY FEAR

One of my favorite portions of Scripture is in 1 John. It reminds us of who we are in Christ. Read it in other translations when you have time. The Amplified Bible brings joy to your heart when you meditate on these verses and realize what they say to you: This passage of Scripture should dispel all the fear you could ever acquire. When you feel fear creeping around you, start quoting this verse. Repeat it over and over.

> Little children, you can be certain that you belong to God and have conquered them, for the One who is living in you is far greater than the one who is in the world. … Those who are loved by God, let his love continually pour from you to one another, because God is love. Everyone who loves is fathered by God and experiences an intimate knowledge of him.
> (1 John 4:4, 7 TPT)

Now let's examine some of the things this passage says and apply them to our own lives.

WE ARE OF GOD; WE BELONG TO HIM

If we belong to God, we are His possession. If we are His possession, He is going to take good care of us. We take care of our possessions, don't we? God does the same thing. He cares about a sparrow that falls and even counts the number of hairs on our heads, so naturally He's going to take good care of us. If He's taking care of us, why should we worry about the devil and live in fear? We belong to God; we don't belong to the devil.

You belong to God, and He loves you!

> "What is the value of your soul to God? Could your worth be defined by an amount of money? God doesn't abandon or forget even the small sparrow he

has made. How then could he forget or abandon you? What about the seemingly minor issues of your life? Do they matter to God? Of course they do! So you never need to worry, for you are more valuable to God than anything else in this world." (Luke 12:6–7 TPT)

JESUS LIVES IN US AND IS GREATER THAN ANYTHING OUTSIDE OF US!

One of the things that will strengthen your life more than anything else concerning fear is to be constantly aware of the fact that Jesus is living in you.

Christ in you, the hope of glory. (Colossians 1:27)

Let the Holy Spirit in you rise up and say to the world:

Greater is He that is in me, than he that is in the world! (1 John 4:4 KJV)

Say it over and over and over until it begins to stick to your ribs and becomes embedded in your heart. Say it to God. Say it to yourself. Say it to your family. Say it to the walls. Say it on the telephone every time it rings. Say it in your bathtub. Say it in your bed. Repeat it over and over until you are thoroughly convinced that Jesus lives inside you, the One who is greater and mightier than he that is in the world.

YOU HAVE ALREADY DEFEATED AND OVERCOME THE DEVIL. WHY ARE YOU AFRAID?

If you really love Jesus, your trust in Him will always exceed any fear of the devil. When you confess that you are afraid, you are saying the Word of God is inaccurate and not true. You are denying God's omniscience and what Jesus did on the cross for you. You need to know what God's Word says so you can firmly plant your two feet on it and stand in faith.

The Bible says you have already defeated and overcome the devil. How can you be concerned and full of worry if you believe what God's Word tells you? His Word plainly says that you have already overcome. Act on what you believe in: God's Word, truth, love, and protection.

Rebuke the devil-instilled fear. Place your faith in God. He can perform what He says.

> But we belong to God, and whoever truly knows God listens to us. Those who refuse to listen to us do not belong to God. That is how we can know the difference between the spirit of truth and the spirit of deceit. (1 John 4:6 TPT)

WE ARE CHILDREN OF GOD

This is another wonderful key to finding freedom from fear. Understand that you are a child of God. Know it, know it, know it! How do you know it? By getting to know Him better. How do we get to know Him better? By reading His Word over and over and over.

Everything you read in His Word points to His love and care for you, but you won't ever know this until you read it and get it firmly fixed in your heart and mind.

Mom went home to heaven when she was ninety-two. She once explained, "I think of all the years I lived in this world, attended church, and had a precious Bible. I wanted to take such good care of my Bible that I never used it for fear I'd wear it out. No wonder I didn't know what God had for me. I never bothered to find out. I was starving to death spiritually even though His whole basket of goodies was right there waiting for me to eat!"

Beloved, let us love one another, for love is of God; and everyone who loves is born of God and knows God. (1 John 4:7)

Notice the words "born of God" and "knows God" mentioned in this verse. To dispel fear, get as close to God as possible by spending time with Him in His Word and in prayer.

When Mom first became a Christian, she read the Bible until two or three in the morning. Even at work, she would concentrate on the Word of God and feel the love that was pouring into her while she was getting acquainted with Him.

That first awakening to God's love can be the most beautiful time in your life. Being so immersed in the precious Word of God, you will feel totally possessed by His wonderful love.

There is no short cut to knowing God and experiencing and feeling His love. Welcome Him into your heart! Allow His love to flow into and through you. By doing this, you will overcome fear that involves torment.

A woman called my mom on the telephone one day and asked for prayer. Mom asked her what her problem was. Her answer was: "Many!" She began to name a whole string of diagnoses which involved her whole body.

Mom asked, "What are you afraid of? Why are you so fearful?"

Mom knew it wouldn't do any good to minister healing to her body until the underlying cause was identified and removed. Every affliction this lady had was caused by some form of fear. After talking with her for a while, the lady realized her problem had come from listening to the lies of the devil. The enemy always wants to grab your mind and thoughts.

This woman had received the baptism with the Holy Spirit three years previously in a glorious experience. Then the devil came around and told her the baptism wasn't real. As a result of this lie, she had lived in fear of speaking in tongues or associating with anyone who did. Because she thought it was of the devil, she was afraid to open her mouth and praise God in her prayer language.

The devil had told her for three years that she couldn't pray in tongues. She became completely convinced that it was an impossibility for her. She had been unbelievably depressed for three long years of defeat because she failed to depend and stand on the Word of God.

With a short, simple command, Mom cast out the spirit of fear. Immediately, the lady started praying in tongues as the joy of the Lord came over her! The worst fear in the whole world is the fear that attaches itself to you. It might seem like nothing or insignificant to someone else; however, when fear has hooked its claws into you, regardless of what it is, it will become a huge, overwhelming, overpowering force in your life until you learn what God has to say about fear.

That is just one testimony about fear. I could tell you many more. Fear is rampant today. The enemy is busy serving a huge platter of torment all around the world. Spread the Word!

FAITH IN GOD CONQUERS FEAR!

Quote these words from a very well-known Psalm written by David:

> The Lord is my shepherd; I shall not want. He maketh me to lie down in green pastures: he leadeth me beside the still waters. He restoreth my soul: he leadeth me in the paths of righteousness for his

name's sake. Yea, though I walk through the valley of the shadow of death, I will fear no evil: for thou art with me; thy rod and thy staff they comfort me. Thou preparest a table before me in the presence of mine enemies: thou anointest my head with oil; my cup runneth over. Surely goodness and mercy shall follow me all the days of my life: and I will dwell in the house of the Lord for ever. (Psalm 23 KJV)

In fact, you need to memorize these powerful words. Whenever you feel fear trying to sneak into any area of your life, quote it over and over. Bury it deep in your heart and spirit.

David said, "I will fear no evil." Why and how could he say that with such confidence? "For You are with me," he proclaimed in that same Psalm. David stood on the promises of God and refused to fear *any* evil.

You may say, "But David was never surrounded with the bad situation I'm in." You may argue that his problems never compared with yours. Are you sure of that?

Why wasn't he afraid? He gives his answer in Psalm 3:

But you, O Lord, are a shield around me; you are my glory, the one who holds my head high. I cried out to the Lord, and he answered me from his holy mountain. I lay down and slept, yet I woke up in safety, for the Lord was watching over me.

I am not afraid of ten thousand enemies who surround me on every side. Arise, O Lord! Rescue me, my God! Slap all my enemies in the face! Shatter the teeth of the wicked! (Psalm 3:3–7 NLT)

David really loved God and showed it by trusting Him. Have you ever had ten thousand enemies surround you on every side trying to kill you? Then your problem couldn't be as bad as David's was. He simply gave the problem to God and went to sleep. Most of us would have stayed awake all night worrying, but David knew that God heard his cries for help. He just went to bed and relaxed. That's the greatest way to get rid of fear that I know of—just give it to God and then let Him handle the problem.

Another Scripture concerning fear is found in Exodus 14. Moses had led the Israelites out of Egypt and the Egyptian army was chasing them. Watching Pharaoh's army getting closer with every minute, they complained and murmured to Moses. They were just plain scared!

> And Moses said to the people: "Do not be afraid. Stand still, and see the salvation of the Lord, which He will accomplish for you today. For the Egyptians whom you see today, you shall see again no more forever. The Lord will fight for you, and you shall hold your peace." (Exodus 14:13–14)

Moses was really saying, "Put your trust in God! Don't look at the problem!" They didn't realize that not only was God on the scene already, but His warrior angels were also there to defeat the foe and protect them.

Verse 15 finally tells them what else to do to survive and get the victory:

> "Tell the children of Israel to go forward."

In today's language, we would say, "Forward, march!" God's answer was a plan that involved action. He didn't want them to just sit there and wait for disaster to overtake them. He wanted them to get moving toward complete victory.

You need to do the same thing. Let God answer your prayers

and then get moving out of the realm of fear into the realm of faith. God will never let you down when you are doing what He tells you to do!

Too often people sit and complain instead of moving out for and with God. Give Him an opportunity to solve the problems. God is not on the defensive. God is on the offensive. God likes action.

The devil tries his delay tactics all the time. Watch the next time you are doing something for God. The devil's favorite trick is distraction. He wants you to sit down and cry. He wants you to talk to all your friends about every negative event that has happened or will happen. Make your choice: whine or believe God.

Praise God for His promises of the future and what it holds for you. Know who holds the future! Follow God! Forward, march!

THE DEVIL DELAYS: GOD MOVES!

Probably the greatest fear in the world today is the fear of failure. If I asked the congregation during a meeting if anyone was afraid of poverty, old age, cancer, or losing a husband or wife, many people would raise their hand. If I continue with the question, "How many of you have a fear of failure?" most hands would be held high in the air.

It is always surprising that Christians admit they have a fear of failure. The greatest weapon against fear is the Word of God. Be determined to sharpen that two-edged sword.

> For we have the living Word of God, which is full of energy, and it pierces more sharply than a two-edged sword. It will even penetrate to the very core of our being where soul and spirit, bone and marrow meet! It interprets and reveals the true thoughts and secret motives of our hearts. (Hebrews 4:12 TPT)

ANNIHILATE FEAR

When you keep that sword sharp, you can chop fear into tiny little pieces and God will scatter the refuse to the four winds. Fear has no right to be in the heart of a believer! Those who are fearful often blame a lack of time for not spending time in the Word of God and learning the promises they can stand on. Instead, they will take all the time in the world to discuss their fears with anyone who will listen.

> And never let ugly or hateful words come from your mouth, but instead let your words become beautiful gifts that encourage others; do this by speaking words of grace to help them. (Ephesians 4:29 TPT)

> So keep your thoughts continually fixed on all that is authentic and real, honorable and admirable, beautiful and respectful, pure and holy, merciful and kind. And fasten your thoughts on every glorious work of God, praising him always. (Philippians 4:8 TPT)

Listen to yourself when you speak to other people. Are you sharing encouragement or pouring negativity on them? Yes, there are so many serious concerns plaguing today's world. The "worldview" is scary and destructive. Talking like the world will drag you down to where the enemy wants you. Fear comes into your life when you don't know your actual inheritance from God.

How much better for the hearers when you let them know who you are in Christ! The minute you discover who you are, you will begin to have victory over fear. Sickness, anxiety, and failure will all fade away when God is allowed to monopolize your conversation.

Try something. Get a piece of paper right now and write down all the fears you have in your life. Make the list as long as you need to. Write down every one of your fears, big and small. At the bottom of the page, write in big, bold letters:

> Yet even in the midst of all these things, we triumph over them all, for God has made us to be more than conquerors, and his demonstrated love is our glorious victory over everything! (Romans 8:37 TPT)

When you've finished your list, crumble it up in your hand. You might want to stomp on it while you quote that verse loudly at the devil. Before you are done, you might even want to burn the list. Let the devil know those fears don't exist anymore!

God's Word doesn't allow room for failure. Over and over, He gives us the prescription for total deliverance from fear and worry.

Another of my favorite Scriptures as an antidote to fear of failure is in the Amplified Bible. Imagine yourself obeying His Word.

> Roll your works upon the Lord—commit and trust them wholly to Him; [He will cause your thoughts to become agreeable to His will, and] so shall your plans be established and succeed. (Proverbs 16:3 AMP)

Did you ever go bowling or watch someone else bowl? You use a ball which has three holes for your fingers and thumb. You stand at one end of a long wooden freeway and try to knock down the pins at the other end of the lane. Everyone gets excited when you knock them all down. The secret in bowling is to release the ball right down the center path (with a slight curve) and it's done!

My point? You can't knock the pins down with the ball still in your hand.

The same secret holds true in "rolling your works upon the

Lord." You must "let go" of the load you've been carrying and throw everything on the Lord. Turn it loose!

The next step is important. "Commit and trust them wholly to Him." Isn't that difficult sometimes? After we've let go, we begin to wonder if we can trust God for the answers.

Have you ever felt like you wanted to run down the alley after the bowling ball? That's what a lot of us do with problems. We give them to God and then run after them as fast as we can to take them back.

Years ago, some young people did a skit at church. Each of them wrote their sins and problems on a piece of paper. In front of everyone, they each boldly threw their lists into a garbage can and confidently walked away cheering in victory. They all left the stage. Everything was silent and still for several minutes.

One by one, each young person came sneaking from various directions of the church back to the garbage can. They dug through the mess to find their own piece of paper. Showing obvious sorrow and shame, they each hid their "list" in a pocket and crawled away in defeat.

The Bible is so simple and specific in telling us to commit and trust our problems "wholly" to Him—not just halfway, but all the way! Watch what happens when you do.

> Commit your works to the Lord, and your thoughts will be established. (Proverbs 16:3)

Do you see what happens when you give your mind, your fears, and your works to God? Working in agreement with God brings a wonderful promise—a secret for success! If you believe the Word of God to be true and obey what it says, there is no way you can be a failure. God's Word promises that your plans shall be established and succeed.

Failure and success don't go together. Fear and faith aren't dating either.

God said in Genesis 26:24,

> "Fear not for I am with you, and will favor you with blessings" (AMP).

The Living Bible adds "because of my promise."

He can be trusted! He will be with each of His children! He is true to His wonderful Word! One of the most beautiful antidotes for the fear of failure is found in the first chapter of Psalms.

> And he shall be like a tree planted by the rivers of water, that bringeth forth his fruit in his season; his leaf also shall not wither; and whatsoever he doeth shall prosper. (Psalms 1:3 KJV)

Years ago, a group called "The Amigos" traveled with Mom and Dad. One day in the back of the bus, this Psalm was turned into a song. Once anyone heard it, the tune and words would run through their memories. Often, someone would be humming or singing the tune.

"I am like a tree planted by the streams of water…" We would end it with "Everything I do shall prosper. Everything I say will prosper. Everything I touch shall prosper. Everyone I touch will prosper."

How can we ever anticipate failure when God's Word promises us that everything we do is going to prosper? We need to confess that over and over until we have prosperity rolling in our doors in such great measure that we don't have room to contain it. That's God's way. That's what God wants.

If success is what you need, take God's prescription as listed in Deuteronomy.

ANNIHILATE FEAR

"Look, the Lord your God has set the land before you; go up and possess it, as the Lord God of your fathers has spoken to you; do not fear or be discouraged." (Deuteronomy 1:21)

That's an order from God! He's ordering you to go out and possess the things He has for you. He's saying to you, "Go get your inheritance. Go possess what I've given to you. Go get what is rightfully yours!"

God gives simple instructions. He tells you that you are not to fear and neither are you to be discouraged. Don't tell God you don't believe what He says, and that you are going to be disobedient. Begin confessing God's Word! When the day comes that you learn to confess the Word of God instead of the lies of Satan, it will be a great day of victory for you and a great day of rejoicing for the Lord.

If God be for us, who can be against us? (Romans 8:31)

It doesn't make any difference who is against you because you are saved from the enemy and are now a child of the King!

That if you confess with your mouth the Lord Jesus and believe in your heart that God has raised Him from the dead, you will be saved. For with the heart one believes unto righteousness, and with the mouth confession is made unto salvation.
 For the Scripture says, "Whoever believes on Him will not be put to shame." For there is no distinction between Jew and Greek, for the same Lord over all is rich to all who call upon Him. For "whoever calls on the name of the Lord shall be saved." (Romans 10:9–13)

Confession is made unto success or failure, whichever you choose. Confessing fear will bring fear. Confessing God's Word will make the Bible a reality. If you line up your life with the Word of God, the Word of God will line up with your life!

> Say to them that are of a fearful heart, Be strong, fear not: behold, your God will come and save you.
> (Isaiah 35:4 KJV)

That's a personal word from the Lord just for you! Where does fear start?

Many times, we instill fear in our children as it was once instilled in us, and then it continues throughout their lifetime. Some parents have said to their children, "Watch out or the boogeyman will get you!" Or maybe, "If you don't behave, I'll put you in the dark!" Darkness then becomes a thing to fear. Telling ghost stories was the "in" thing when Mom was growing up. Everyone tried to come up with the most gory, gruesome story possible to scare everybody else. In those days, kids put a value and excitement on fear.

When my oldest daughter, Charity, was about two years old, many of the children in the neighborhood came by on Halloween dressed in costumes grotesque enough to scare even the calmest individual. When Charity became frightened and ran behind me, I calmly said, "Honey, you don't have to be afraid because the angels have charge over thee, to keep thee in all thy ways." What a confession for a two-year-old child to learn!

> For He shall give His angels charge over you, to keep you in all your ways. (Psalm 91:11)

The Passion Translations says it this way:

ANNIHILATE FEAR

God sends angels with special orders to protect you wherever you go, defending you from all harm.

To this day, Charity has no fear because she knows what the Bible says. She now teaches her children to say, "The angels have charge over me!" That's the confession you need to make. When the devil tries to put fear in you, confess the protection of the angels over yourself. Don't confess the devil's power; confess God's Word!

Someone gave Mom and Dad some Bible markers that had twenty-two different-colored ribbons. They laid them down on their desk. When Charity visited, she immediately spotted them, put some in each hand, and started running through the house with the ribbons flying in the air as she said, "He's alive! He's alive! He's alive!"

As young as she was, her thoughts were on Jesus! She'll never think of Jesus as dead. To her, "He's alive!" How we wish that all Christians would excitedly proclaim the same message with banners flying. Somewhere in her mind had been imprinted the fact that *He's alive!*

Fear exists when you don't sincerely and honestly believe that Jesus is alive and capable of handling all of your affairs better than you could. Doubt and the devil go hand in hand. When doubt comes in, you don't think God is big enough to take care of you, so fear traps you where the devil wants you.

Fear is the absence of trust in God. If you really love Jesus, you will not live in fear.

When you have been raised in and have lived in an atmosphere of fear, how do you get over it, especially when you are past your childhood days? There's only one way I know that is guaranteed to work. Start confessing and possessing the Word of God. Fear of not knowing your standing with God can be so easily taken care of by a simple prayer.

Repeat this right now: "Father, I have things in my life that make me afraid of my eternal destiny. Please forgive my sins and cleanse me. I promise to quit doing anything displeasing to You as soon as I know it is wrong. I know You will let me know in my heart instantly when I am not pleasing You. Thank You for forgiving me and thank You for the peace You promise when I obey You. In Jesus' name. Amen."

Where do you go from here? The answer is simple. Possess the promises of God, so, like God told the children of Israel, you can go in and possess the land. Pray this prayer: "I believe You want me to possess my rights as Your child, Father. Right now, by faith, I possess peace. I rebuke all fear, especially the fear of death. I have the power and desire to obey Your every wish, and therefore I have full rights as Your child to enjoy total peace and freedom from all fear! I love You! In Jesus' name. Amen."

HEALTHY FEAR

The Bible distinguishes between two kinds of fear. One is the negative fear we have talked about, but the other is necessary fear—godly fear. This fear is reverence toward God, an attitude of awe and wonder at God's greatness and His marvelous ways. It means to honor, obey, respect, reverence, and worship Him.

The Holy Spirit reveals God as our loving Father, and a holy fear (or respect) of God is the result of our walking "in truth." This type of fear is not the frightening kind of fear but is connected only with respect or awe. When we have this fear (or awe) of God, we possess peace, joy, contentment, and serenity. God seeks only good for His children and certainly nothing evil.

Years ago, many evangelists and pastors preached "hellfire

and brimstone." In other words, they wanted to scare you into heaven. If you didn't run to the altar and "get saved," you would burn in hell. Scaring people into heaven is not from God.

To be afraid of God means we don't really know and understand Him, or that we are rebelling against Him and have reason to be afraid. This negative fear destroys the peace we could possess. When sin in our lives creates fear in us, the thing to do is confess that sin to God and ask forgiveness for it right then and there.

> If we confess our sins, He is faithful and just to forgive us our sins and to cleanse us from all unrighteousness. (1 John 1:9 NLT)

To continue living in rebellion puts us in constant fear of what would happen to us if we died. Psychologists say that fear of death is one of the most common fears known to man. It is not actually the fear of death itself, but fear of what will happen to us after we die.

The word *possess* means to have, to hold, to occupy, to enjoy, to own, to command, to inherit, to acquire, to retain, to belong to, to pertain to, to be in one's possession. You need to *possess* God's Word.

You need to have God's promises in your heart, to hold onto them with your spirit, and to let them occupy your thoughts so you can enjoy life. When you possess the promises of God, you can speak them boldly with full confidence, because you have inherited, through salvation, all of God's promises. You have acquired and will retain them because they belong to you and are in your possession as long as you act upon them.

> Words kill, words give life; they're either poison or fruit—you choose. (Proverbs 18:21 MSG)

GOD IS FOR ME!

One of the best confessions against fear (which I would recommend you memorize) is found in Psalm 27:

> The Lord is my light and my salvation; whom shall I fear? The Lord is the strength of my life; of whom shall I be afraid?
> When the wicked came against me to eat up my flesh, my enemies and foes, they stumbled and fell. My heart shall not fear; though war may rise against me, in this I will be confident. One thing I have desired of the Lord, that will I seek: that I may dwell in the house of the Lord all the days of my life, to behold the beauty of the Lord, and to inquire in His temple.
> For in the time of trouble He shall hide me in His pavilion; in the secret place of His tabernacle He shall hide me; He shall set me high upon a rock. And now my head shall be lifted up above my enemies all around me; therefore I will offer sacrifices of joy in His tabernacle; I will sing, yes, I will sing praises to the Lord. (Psalm 27:1–6)

You have *nothing, nothing, nothing* to fear!

> "Behold, I give you the authority to trample on serpents and scorpions, and over all the power of the enemy, and nothing shall by any means hurt you." (Luke 10:19)

Say that over and over and over until it is as much a part of you as your eyes. Then you will know that nothing shall by any means hurt you. The Bible promises that *nothing* shall hurt you. Fear can't reach you as long as you are believing and living by the Word of God.

ANNIHILATE FEAR

You may have heard about word curses. These are negative, evil words spoken to you or over you that can bring on fear. These words can easily and quickly be rebuked in Jesus' name. Do not let them take up residence in your mind or heart. In other words, don't invite them in!

> An undeserved curse will be powerless to harm you. It may flutter over you like a bird, but it will find no place to land. (Proverbs 26:2 TPT)

> "For by your words you will be justified, and by your words you will be condemned." (Matthew 12:37)

It's amazing how your mouth can lead you right into the pit of hell through fear. If you speak fear, you will be full and overflowing with horrible, condemning fear. Those same lips can form the right words and you will be justified. Hallelujah! Be careful of the things of God. Freedom from fear comes so easily if you will listen and obey the words of Jesus.

> Jesus said to those Jews who believed in him, "When you continue to embrace all that I teach, you prove that you are my true followers. For if you embrace the truth, it will release more freedom into your lives." (John 8:31–32 TPT)

Nothing but the truth can set you free. To find that freedom, stay in His Word at all times. I love the words of an old favorite hymn, "Standing On the Promises." It says, "Standing on the promises that cannot fail, when the howling storms of doubt and fear assail."

Christians walking in doubt often say, "Will God really do this? Will God really do that?" Remember, you can stand on the promises of God. Don't look at the circumstances, look at Jesus, because God's Word has never failed!

> The power of God caused the word to spread, and the people were greatly impacted. (Acts 19:20 TPT)

When you hide the Word of God in your heart, that Word is going to grow, and grow, and grow until His Word is victorious over your circumstances. You can look at situations that don't look good, but if you stand on His promises, His promises will come true. Remember, anything that is not of faith is sin.

> For anything we do that doesn't spring from faith is, by definition, sinful. (Romans 14:23 TPT)

Is fear of faith? No, fear and faith are complete opposites of each other. If fear remains in your life, it is sin! No one wants to sin, so agree with God that His perfect love casts out *all* fear.

My parents were visiting a Canadian church years ago. Nobody knew they were going to be there. The pastor had just extended an invitation to them the day before, and they agreed because they were free that Sunday morning. When they walked in, the pastor asked Dad to go someplace with him.

Mom was left alone for a few minutes in the narthex of the church. As she was standing there looking out the door at the deep snow, one of the ushers walked up, introduced himself, and said, "There is an aura that surrounds you. I saw it when you walked in." He paused a moment, and then continued, "You really know who you are, don't you?"

She smiled and responded, "I certainly do know who I am in Christ! I have overcome the devil by the blood of the Lamb and by the word of my testimony. I am a joint heir with Jesus. The Lord is my shepherd, and I shall not want for anything. Greater is He that is in me than he that is in the world. I'm a child of the King. That's who I am."

Praise God, Jesus' love just glowed from my mom. Christians should not be cringing slaves of fear. You need to throw your shoulders back and let the world know you've got something special and know who you are. You are nothing by yourself, but you are everything in Christ.

When you know exactly who you are in Christ, that knowledge will drive fear right off the scene. Here are some words that will warm your heart. Read aloud this song by King David composed after his escape from King Saul. You can just feel David's enthusiasm in God's power and love.

> Lord! I'm bursting with joy over what you've done for me! My lips are full of perpetual praise. I'm boasting of you and all your works, so let all who are discouraged take heart. Join me, everyone! Let's praise the Lord together. Let's make him famous! Let's make his name glorious to all.
>
> Listen to my testimony: I cried to God in my distress and he answered me. He freed me from all my fears! Gaze upon him, join your life with his, and joy will come. Your faces will glisten with glory. You'll never wear that shame-face again. When I had nothing, desperate and defeated, I cried out to the Lord and he heard me, bringing his miracle-deliverance when I needed it most. (Psalm 34:1–6 TPT)

Anytime you start feeling down, you should really read the entire chapter. It is powerful. If the praise of God is continually in your mouth, you can't be shouting the praises of the devil, can you? When you walk and talk fear, you're just shouting the praises of the devil and telling the world that he is greater than God. My God is greater!

Who are you going to boast about? The devil or God? You can't do both, and if you're busy telling the world what the Lord has done for you, you won't have time to tell them about the fear that is trying to creep into your life.

Get someone to magnify the Lord with you. Praise His name! If you don't, Satan will have hundreds of cohorts ready to sympathize and agree with you in a pity party of fear.

God promises if you seek Him, talk to Him, and praise Him, He will deliver you. Boast and brag to your friends about what the Lord is doing or has done in your life, and He will elevate you to a place of victory.

In Jesus, you will experience deliverance from *all* fears. Read this special message written just for you out of the Amplified Bible:

> Oh, how great is Your goodness, which You have laid up for those who fear, revere, and worship You, goodness which You have wrought for those who trust and take refuge in You before the sons of men! In the secret place of Your presence You hide them from the plots of men; You keep them secretly in Your pavilion from the strife of tongues. (Psalm 31:19–20 AMP)

Hallelujah, I am secretly hidden in God; nothing can get to me! Another great Scripture for any person who is troubled with fear is found in 2 Timothy:

> For God has not given us the spirit of fear; but of power, and of love, and of a sound mind. (2 Timothy 1:7)

Repeat this verse over and over and over until you possess

it. That's what God's Word has to say about fear. What has God given us? What are we to possess?

POWER, LOVE, AND A SOUND MIND

Power...authority, might, and strength from God (Luke 4:6; 2 Corinthians 4:7)...from on high (Luke 24:49)...to become the sons of God (John 1:12). That works in us to perform exceeding and abundant things (Ephesians 3:20)...that destroyed Satan who once had the power of death (Hebrews 2:14)...that keeps us through our faith (1 Peter 1:4–5)...which gives to us all things that pertain to life and godliness through knowing (there's the need to know) Him (2 Peter 1:3)...over the nations. That means over everything in our world or life.

> And he who overcomes and keeps My works until the end, to him will I give power. (Revelation 2:26)

GOD IS LOVE

> God is love! Those who are living in love are living in God, and God lives through them. By living in God, love has been brought to its full expression in us So that we may fearlessly face the day of judgment, because all that Jesus now is, so are we in this world. Love never brings fear, for fear is always related to punishment. But love's perfection drives the fear of punishment far from our hearts. Whoever walks constantly afraid of punishment has not reached love's perfection.
>
>   Our love for others is our grateful response to the love God first demonstrated to us. Anyone can say, "I love God," yet have hatred toward another believer. This makes him a phony, because if you don't love a

brother or sister, whom you can see, how can you truly love God, whom you can't see? For he has given us this command: whoever loves God must also demonstrate love to others. (1 John 4:7–21 TPT)

Mind…we have the sound mind of Christ (1 Corinthians 2:16). God shall keep your heart and mind through Christ Jesus, our Lord (Philippians 4:7).

There are other verses to reference. What are they? Look them up. See how many you can find. Write them down, share them with someone. The words *fear not* are mentioned 355 times in the Bible, one for almost every day of the year. Here are a few of them:

"Fear not, for I am with you; Be not dismayed, for I am your God. I will strengthen you, Yes, I will help you, I will uphold you with my righteous right hand." (Isaiah 43:1)

Also I said to you, "I am the Lord your God; do not fear the gods of the Amorites (heathen, the pagans, the enemy), in whose land you dwell." (Judges 6:10)

Then the Lord said to Joshua: "Do not be afraid, nor be dismayed; take all the people of war with you, and arise, go up." (Joshua 8:1)

And when I saw Him, I fell at His feet as dead. But He laid His right hand on me, saying to me, "Do not be afraid; I am the First and the Last. I am He who lives, and was dead, and behold, I am alive forevermore. Amen. And I have the keys of Hades and of Death." (Revelation 1:17–18)

ANNIHILATE FEAR

> Do not fear, little flock, for it is your Father's good pleasure to give you the kingdom. (Luke 12:32)
>
> Fear not, O land; Be glad and rejoice, For the Lord has done marvelous things. Do not be afraid. (Joel 2:21–22)

This short list only shows a few of the many verses about fear that appear in the Bible. That should give you an idea of what God is saying to you: "Fear not, fear not, fear not! Don't be afraid, trust Me."

> Don't be afraid. Just stand where you are and watch and you will see the wonderful way the Lord will rescue you today. (Exodus 14:13 TLB)
>
> Listen to my testimony: I cried to God in my distress and he answered me. He freed me from all my fears! (Psalm 34:4 TPT)

He's telling you to hang loose and don't get paralyzed with fear. When you're afraid of failure, read 1 Chronicles 28:20:

> Then he continued, "Be strong and courageous and get to work. Don't be frightened by the size of the task, for the Lord my God is with you; he will not forsake you. He will see to it that everything is finished correctly." (TLB)
>
> God is our refuge and strength, a very present help in trouble. Therefore we will not fear, even though the earth be removed, and though the mountains be carried into the midst of the sea; though its waters roar and be troubled, though the mountains shake with its swelling. Selah.

GOD IS FOR ME!

> There is a river whose streams shall make glad the city of God, the holy place of the tabernacle of the Most High. God is in the midst of her, she shall not be moved; God shall help her, just at the break of dawn.
> The Lord of hosts is with us; the God of Jacob is our refuge. Selah. ... Be still, and know that I am God; I will be exalted among the nations, I will be exalted in the earth! The Lord of hosts is with us; the God of Jacob is our refuge. Selah. (Psalm 46:1–5, 7, 10–11)

Praise the Lord. We don't even have to worry if the world blows up with a bomb and the whole earth falls into the sea. Hallelujah! God says that He will be in our midst and we have nothing to fear. Did you ever have everything go wrong at one time? Well, I did, and maybe this story will deliver you from the fear that the devil will win your battle.

My parents had a bad day years ago. It seemed like their world was falling apart. Problems in the office, the loan for the new building was held up at the bank, and the devil was having a field day. They sat outside the bank in the car and cried out to God, "God, have you forgotten all about us? What have we done that You don't answer our prayers anymore? Is there something wrong with us? We can hardly pray. God, where are You?"

Mom started the car to drive across town, and the tape recorder automatically came on in the car. She heard her own voice reading Psalm 77:

> I cry to the Lord; I call and call to him. Oh, that he would listen. I am in deep trouble and I need his help so badly. All night long I pray, lifting my hands to heaven, pleading. There can be no joy for me until

> he acts. I think of God and moan, overwhelmed with
> longing for his help. I cannot sleep until you act.
>
> I am too destressed even to pray! I keep thinking of the good old days of the past long since ended. Then my nights were filled with joyous songs. I search my soul and meditate upon the difference now. Has the Lord rejected me forever? Will he never again be favorable? Is his loving kindness gone forever? Has his promise failed? Has he forgotten to be kind to one so undeserving? Has he slammed the door in anger on his love? And I said: This is my fate, that the blessings of God have changed to hate.
>
> I recall the many miracles he did for me so long ago. Those wonderful deeds are constantly in my thoughts, I cannot stop thinking about them. (TLB)

These were the very words Mom had just cried out to God. They were the same words David cried out, and the same words Jesus cried out as He went to the cross.

God knew what she needed! The cassette came to the end and she flipped it over. Guess what came on next?

> The very day I call for help, the tide of battle turns.
> My enemies flee! This one thing I know; God is for me!
> I am trusting God—oh, praise his promises.
> (Psalm 56:9 TLB)

Mom got so excited. God was reassuring her that the tide of the battle had turned. He was assuring her that there was no reason for her to be afraid because He was for her. He was for them. He was for Hunter Ministries. Hallelujah!

The tide of the battle did turn. God smoothed out the problems, and everything started going ahead full speed.

GOD IS FOR ME!

> For God has not given us a spirit of fear, but of power and of love and of a sound mind. (2 Timothy 1:7)

The fear of everything going wrong immediately left Mom when she heard her own voice coming from the tape recorder, saying, "This one thing I know—God is for me!"

Nothing, nothing, *nothing* can take the place of the Word of God when you're having problems. Are you His child today? Then He is for you.

Say it aloud!

GOD IS FOR ME!

GOD IS FOR ME!

GOD IS FOR ME!

GOD IS FOR ME!

GOD IS FOR ME!

"**GOD IS FOR ME!**"

3

DEVIL, YOU CAN'T STEAL MY PEACE!

Satan comes to steal your joy, your peace, your comfort, your finances, your salvation, your health! He comes to steal *everything* that you hold precious. Know how to recognize his tricks designed to fool you into obeying him instead of listening to God.

> "The thief cometh not, but for to steal, and to kill, and to destroy: I am come that they might have life, and that they might have it more abundantly." (John 10:10 KJV)

Have you been listening to the enemy? If you truly want to belong to God's family and be eligible for His protection and all His promises, repeat this prayer right now before you go any further: "Father, I want to be part of Your family. I am tired of fighting the world system and lies by myself. I need You. Please forgive me, Father, for all the things I have messed up doing things my way. I choose Your way today. I want Jesus and Your precious Holy Spirit to live within me. I accept Jesus as Your Son and my Savior. Open my eyes to Your ways and Your Word. In Jesus' name. Amen."

How can you know or understand anything about God's peace, joy, love, happiness, contentment, prosperity, and abundant life? Because you read the Word of God. The Bible was written under God's direction. He did not leave man alone to guess how to survive. He left you the instruction manual to live successfully on earth: the Holy Bible.

OVERCOMING FEAR

The minute the Word of God gets into your heart, you begin to understand the promises of God and how to live under His guidance. The devil then does his best to steal the Word away. God has given man the gift of choice. You have to make the decision to choose God's way or follow the lies of the enemy.

We put much emphasis on reading the Word, speaking the Word, believing the Word, and standing on His promises with faith. Once you get your spirit-man full of the Word of God, the devil is going to have a difficult time attracting you down his path to destruction.

The Word of God hidden deep within your heart will allow you to rise above the negative situations in life.

> Be well balanced and always alert, because your enemy, the devil, roams around incessantly, like a roaring lion looking for its prey to devour. (1 Peter 5:8 TPT)

This is a battle between good and evil. Satan doesn't give up trying to entice God's children to turn their backs on their Father and embrace his lies that lead to certain death and defeat. Unfortunately, the devil's antics are not difficult to recognize these days.

DEVIL, YOU CAN'T STEAL MY PEACE!

We will see more of the devil's influence before Jesus comes back than ever before.

> "A sower went out to sow his seed: and as he sowed, some fell by the wayside; and it was trodden down, and the fowls of the air devoured it. And some fell upon a rock; and as soon as it was sprung up, it withered away, because it lacked moisture."
> (Luke 8:5–6 KJV)

What's the moisture that you need in your life? The moisture is the living water of life! It comes in to water your inner spirit by a continuation of *reading* and *believing* the Word of God. You need to fertilize it so the Word that's in you will continue to grow.

> "And some fell among the thorns; and the thorns sprang up with it and choked it. And others fell on the good ground, and sprang up, and bare fruit a hundredfold." And when He had said these things, He cried, "He that hath ears to hear, let him hear."
> And the disciples said to him, "What might this parable be?" And He said, "Unto you it is given to know the mysteries of the kingdom of God: but to others in parables; that seeing they might not see and hearing they might not understand."
> Then He said, "Now the parable is this: The seed is the Word of God. Those by the wayside are they that hear; then cometh the devil, and taketh away the Word out of their hearts, lest they should believe and be saved." (Luke 8:7–15 KJV)

The powerful seed that the devil wants to steal from you is the

Word of God. The minute you begin to hear the Word, the devil is going to be right there to steal that Word out of your heart so that you no longer believe in or want to follow Jesus.

I like to say it this way: "Faith cometh by hearing, and hearing, and hearing, and hearing, and hearing the Word of God." The Word of God will never stay in your heart if you hear it only one time. You need to keep replenishing that supply.

The same thing is true of food. We could not exist if we ate one meal this year and didn't eat another until next year. Some of us might do a little better with fewer meals, but we all know that there is no way you can get along without physical food. You have to nourish your body.

When God created us, His plan included our eating physical food regularly to keep our bodies both alive and healthy. To keep our spirits alive, we need to read the Bible because the most important food in the world is the living Word of God.

I often think about the nations around the world where people are starving to death. What is their main problem? If they could just hear the Word of God, they could be delivered from the poverty, sickness, disease, sin, and death in which they now live. The lack of the Word of God keeps them in the mess they are in. You can give them physical food and it will satisfy their stomachs for one day, but what is going to happen the next day? They are going to be hungry all over again.

If they receive the Word of God, they will learn how to be delivered from sin, sickness, poverty, death, and disease. When they understand the principles of God, you won't have to worry that this nation or any other nation is going to have to feed them over and over again.

Jesus came to deliver us from the curse, which includes sin, sickness, poverty, and death!

My mom, best known as Frances Hunter, enjoyed almost

total divine health once she became a Christian. However, every once in a while, the devil sneaked in and punched her with a low blow, and she went down for the count. During one ministry trip, the devil delivered a case of something called the flu, or a viral infection.

As soon as she felt the symptoms developing, she rebuked them in the name of Jesus and kept on moving. She continued speaking, laying hands on the sick and ministering the baptism with the Holy Spirit. However, as soon as Mom and Dad completed a meeting, she would have to go to bed because she was totally and completely exhausted.

Finally, the long trip was over, and they came home. She was still too busy trying to teach in the School of Ministry and getting things ready for their Video Schools. Mom remained exhausted and, as a result, the devil really closed in. One morning when she woke up, her first thought was, *I don't believe this! I must have signed for that package of flu the devil wanted to give me.*

Again, she immediately bound the devil and rebuked all signs of the flu and attempted to get up. She got about as far as the end of her bed, turned around, and lay down again. She thought she should lie down for another thirty minutes until she could recover her strength. At the end of thirty minutes, she repeated the same thing over and over. She got mad at the enemy and rebuked him again. She wasn't going to accept the package of flu he wanted to give her. It didn't seem that he bothered to put his hearing aid in that day because he wasn't hearing a word she said.

She began to cry out to God, praying that God would touch her. She rolled over for another thirty minutes of rest. This same pattern continued all day long. She couldn't recall when she had felt so totally and completely miserable in her entire life.

Dad came home from the office and found her still in bed.

He came into the bedroom and said, "Honey, we received a tape today from somebody in New Zealand. Do you want to listen?"

He turned the tape player on, and as the man began speaking, it seemed like a long finger reached all the way from New Zealand and pointed straight at Mom. He said, "Have you ever had a day when you felt that God didn't hear your prayers?"

She screamed at the cassette recorder as loud as she could, "Yes!" It seemed like the speaker on this tape waited just long enough for her to say yes, then he continued. "If that's your problem, why don't you try praying in tongues for thirty minutes without stopping?"

Mom turned off the tape recorder and looked at Dad. "Charles, did you hear what he said? He said to pray in tongues for thirty minutes, so let's do it!"

They noted the time and began to pray in tongues. She felt so utterly miserable and didn't feel like praying in tongues at all! She forced herself to continue. She knew the Word says that praying in the Spirit edifies the believer.

Within two or three minutes, her spirit-man began to rise up and be edified by her praying in tongues. At the end of thirty minutes, she was so totally edified by the Spirit that she leaped out of bed, ran to the bathroom, took a shower, washed her hair, blow dried it, went back to bed, and slept like a baby all night long.

The next day, Mom and Dad flew to Dallas and appeared on Bob Tilton's television program *Daystar*. They had been invited to do a radio show for two hours and continued on to do a Miracle Service that night. They flew home to Houston early the next day. Instead of being exhausted and tired, Mom was full of supernatural energy.

Within every Spirit-filled believer is an unleashed, limitless reservoir of power. Take the lid off of that power and use it every day. Praying in tongues thirty minutes a day could turn the world upside down! Mom and Dad shared this revelation on their radio programs and at their Miracle Services. They were swamped with testimonies from people sharing miracles that happened as a result of praying thirty minutes a day in tongues.

> I give thanks to God that I speak in tongues more than all of you. (1 Corinthians 14:18 TPT)

Do something special. Show Brother Paul that you can pray in tongues more than he did. Get yourself so edified and so built up in your faith that there will be no holding back. I've learned something else about "confessing" a healing, and it concerns a "more excellent way."

Were you ever flat on your back and insisting at the same time, "By His stripes I am healed"? Did you ever have your checking account down to zero and still confess, "My bills are paid, my mortgage is paid, I have money in the bank. I claim money in my bank account."

I have often confessed those things, but I want to tell you the story about one of Mom's cars as it relates to healing and prosperity, and whatever else is yours as a child of God. Have you allowed the devil to steal from you? I want to show you how to get it back.

Shortly after Mom became a Christian, she bought a new car. It was a special car because she had problems seeing through a normal windshield at night. She had to wait about eight weeks to get the car that enabled her to drive at night without vision problems.

It was a beautiful shade of teal blue-green, and it had everything that anyone could have ever wanted on or in a car. It was beautiful on the outside and elegant on the inside. She loved that car! It was all hers without a mortgage lien against it. She had the title to it. It was bought, paid for, and all hers.

At that time, she owned a printing company that was located in a shopping center mall. The back door opened onto a large parking area specifically for the tenants. Every time she walked from one department to another, Mom could look out the windows at her new car and say, "Thank you, Jesus! Thank you, Jesus! Thank you, Jesus!" It was a super beautiful car, and she was so grateful that it was totally hers because it was completely paid for.

One day as she was going through the office, she looked out the window and saw a strange man driving her beautiful brand-new car out of the parking lot! She could hardly believe her eyes. She looked again, and sure enough, her new car was being driven out of the parking lot right in front of her. She looked again. It was her car. She had the title to it. She had paid cash for it. The title showed that the car was hers. Nobody had any claim on that car, and here was a man driving off in her car! She got mad.

One of the girls in the office was married to a policeman. Mom knew she would know what to do. She screamed, "Toni, somebody is driving off in my new car!" Then she said, "Get in your car. Let's go get him!" This girl had flaming red hair and plenty of zip. They ran out of the office and jumped into her car, and she scratched out down the alley after the thief.

There was a big supermarket across the street. When the thief got over there, he slowed down, so Mom said, "Toni, zip around in front of him, and block him off!"

Mom got out and ran up to the side of her car, stuck her head inside the window right up against the face of the thief driving it and said, "Get out of my car! What do you think you're doing with it?" At the top of her lungs, she screamed, "Get out of my car!"

The thief didn't blink an eye. Neither did she.

DEVIL, YOU CAN'T STEAL MY PEACE!

Mom screamed again, "Did you hear me? I said get out of my car!"

He said, "What makes you think this is your car?"

She said, "What makes me think it's my car? That's my Bible on the seat next to you, and this is my new car." Then she screamed again, "You get out of my car right now!"

He looked at her and said, "What makes you think your name is Frances?"

She thought to herself, *You've got to be kidding! I certainly ought to know what my own name is!* She realized that he was looking in the rearview mirror. He couldn't back up, and he couldn't go forward because Toni had her car in front of him, and he was just stalling for time.

Again, Mom screamed, "Did you hear me? I said get out of that car! It belongs to me!"

She meant business! By that time, the car in back of him pulled out and the path was free, so he backed up Mom's car about sixty miles an hour, turned it around, and roared off down the alley behind the office again. She ran and jumped back into the car with Toni. Like cops and robbers, they took out after him. He got about halfway down the alley when he stopped her car for a second. Then he really took off.

Mom told Toni, "Follow him!" And she did. These two women were racing down an alley going about eighty miles an hour! She had never prayed so hard for a policeman before. There wasn't one anywhere. Mom did have the car's license number, but he eventually lost them.

You may wonder what the point of this story is, but I'm trying to show you that Mom was even willing to be foolish to protect something that was hers. That car didn't belong to him. It was hers! She had worked hard at her printing company to pay for it.

Then this thief came along and tried to steal it from her in broad daylight.

If she had not seen the man taking her car and chased after him, she would never have gotten that car back again. But she knew it was hers, and nobody was going to take it away from her.

Later, as she explained this story to a policeman, he quietly replied, "According to statistics, you should have been dead within thirteen seconds!"

Mom fought the antics of the enemy with confidence and intensity. She stood strongly on this verse from John's Gospel:

> "The thief does not come except to steal, and to kill, and to destroy. I have come that they may have life, and that they may have it more abundantly." (John 10:10)

We need to fight to keep the devil from stealing our health and finances just as hard as Mom fought to keep that man from stealing her car. Many times, we think we have to work hard to get our healing. Many times, we think we have to stretch to get our prosperity. Many times, we think we have to reach out and claim something, when all we have to do is to *protect* and *recover* what rightfully belongs to us.

Everything God is going to do for you has already been done. Everything Jesus Christ is going to do for you has already been done. Don't allow God's blessings to slip through your fingers because you don't understand. You don't have to beg and plead and claim something that was already rightfully yours.

Jesus died on a cross two thousand years ago, and in so doing He gave you a title deed (with no liens attached) to health, wealth, and happiness. It is yours. He paid for it fully, and that deed is free and clear. The Bible is your title deed to healing, health, prosperity, joy, abundant living, and many other things—right now! They

DEVIL, YOU CAN'T STEAL MY PEACE!

are not something that God is going to give to you in the sweet by-and-by. These things belong to you as God's child. Many have allowed the devil to steal these blessings from them. Don't let the enemy steal your goods. Don't allow the enemy to steal your joy. Don't let him steal your health and peace.

The devil came back after Mom had recovered from the flu and he said, "Ha, ha, ha, that praying in tongues didn't work! You got up one day, didn't you? But I got you right back in bed again!"

Mom prayed in tongues again for another thirty minutes. "Devil, healing is mine! Health is mine! It isn't something that I have to pray and ask God to give to me. He's already given it to me! You have tried to steal it, but health is mine! I'm going to protect it!"

The longer I thought about the episode of Mom's stolen car, the more I began to see a real spiritual truth. Mom said, "Satan, you have stolen the last thing from me that you're ever going to steal. You have messed with the finances of this ministry long enough, because Jesus became poor that we might become rich."

Then Mom added, "You have had your hands in the offerings, you have had your hands in the mail that comes in, but you've done it for the last time! Do you remember how I protected that car sixteen years ago? I'm giving you notice right now that today, and from this day on, I am protecting everything that God gave me in salvation in exactly the same way and with the same fervor that I protected that car, because it's mine!"

You don't have to plead and beg for things that have been given to you. You just have to protect them. I know you may have not been protecting your gifts the way they should be protected. It's all been paid for by the blood of Jesus! Every ache, every pain, every bit of sickness has already been taken care of. Don't let the devil steal it from you. Don't listen to or believe demonic lies.

You need to say, "Devil, you are *never* going to steal from me again!" Fight to protect what is yours. God tells you in His Word that the desire in His heart is for you to prosper and to be in health. God tells you that you are going to prosper.

> Beloved, I pray that you may prosper in all things and be in health, just as your soul prospers. (3 John 1:2)

Jesus told me that I've been delivered from everything related to the curse, so I'm going to protect what belongs to me. It's not something that I have to attempt to acquire, it already belongs to me. How do we protect something that belongs to us?

> Yet, Christ paid the full price to set us free from the curse of the law. He absorbed it completely as he became a curse in our place. (Galatians 3:13 TPT)

Money is taken to the bank. When you need it, the bank will give it back to you. You bank for convenience sake, and you believe the bank is trustworthy because all banks are regulated by law and protected by insurance as security.

To protect your home, you have doors and locks to keep out intruders and burglars. Many homes have alarm systems. To protect offices and property, many organizations have night watchmen. Lights burn continually because a thief likes to operate in the dark. Doors and windows are checked nightly to make sure there is no easy way for a thief to enter property, steal, or destroy.

What protection do you have to prevent the devil from stealing what Jesus paid for and gave to you? Jesus is the door to reach your heavenly Father. He is also your greatest security from theft by the devil. Jesus provided a double-lock system for your protection. Not only is He the door, but He gave you the Word of God.

> For the word of God is quick, and powerful, and sharper than any twoedged sword, piercing even

to the dividing asunder of soul and spirit, and of the joints and the marrow, and is a discerner of the thoughts and intents of the heart. (Hebrews 4:12 KJV)

Remember the attacks of the devil often come through the thoughts and intents of your heart. If you have the Word of God hidden in your heart so you might not sin against Him, you can defeat the entrance of the devil into your heart and mind. Knowing God's Word, His laws, and His principles enables you to operate in the nature of God which is a shield from the entrance or attacks of Satan.

Satan tries to enter the door of your life by bringing sickness into your body. The best preventive medicine is the Word of God. When you saturate yourself with God's Word, the devil has difficulty trying to get in. When you're out of the Word of God, you cause cracks in your armor, and the devil sneaks in.

"Now you understand that I have imparted to you all my authority to trample over his kingdom. You will trample upon every demon before you and overcome every power Satan possesses. Absolutely nothing will be able to harm you as you walk in this authority." (Luke 10:19 TPT)

My parents, Charles and Frances Hunter, wrote the book, *How to Heal the Sick*, so ordinary people would know that they have the power to recover what the devil has stolen. You, too, can heal the sick by the power of the Holy Spirit and with the authority that Jesus has given believers.

To protect your children, you keep a watchful eye on them when they are young and unable to protect themselves. As they get older, you lay down certain rules and regulations for them to follow for their own safety and protection. You make sure they eat the right foods and get sufficient rest and sleep until they are mature enough to operate on their own.

To protect your spiritual life, you need to be alert to the built-in burglar alarm which you have been blessed with, the Holy Spirit! Listen to the little nudges from Him. You have the best fool-proof alarm system in the world nestled inside of you, Open your ears and heart to His voice.

Put on the whole armor of God. A soldier never goes to battle without all the protection he can get. You need to do the same thing because you are in a spiritual war where the enemy is fighting to steal every blessing you have received from God. The Word of God will clothe you from head to toe. Once you get His Word buried deep inside your spirit, it will come out of your mouth at all times. God's Spirit is the best protection in the world against Satan!

> Work hard so God can say to you, "Well done." Be a good workman, one who does not need to be ashamed when God examines your work. Know what his Word says and means. (2 Timothy 2:15 TLB)

> Now my beloved ones, I have saved these most important truths for last: Be supernaturally infused with strength through your life-union with the Lord Jesus. Stand victorious with the force of his explosive power flowing in and through you.
>
> Put on God's complete set of armor provided for us, so that you will be protected as you fight against the evil strategies of the accuser! Your hand-to-hand combat is not with human beings, but with the highest principalities and authorities operating in rebellion under the heavenly realms. For they are a powerful

class of demon-gods and evil spirits that hold this dark world in bondage. Because of this, you must wear all the armor that God provides so you're protected as you confront the slanderer, for you are destined for all things and will rise victorious.

Put on truth as a belt to strengthen you to stand in triumph. Put on holiness as the protective armor that covers your heart. Stand on your feet alert, then you'll always be ready to share the blessings of peace.

In every battle, take faith as your wrap-around shield, for it is able to extinguish the blazing arrows coming at you from the Evil One! Embrace the power of salvation's full deliverance, like a helmet to protect your thoughts from lies. And take the mighty razor-sharp Spirit-sword of the spoken Word of God.

Pray passionately in the Spirit, as you constantly intercede with every form of prayer at all times. Pray the blessings of God upon all his believers. (Ephesians 6:10–18 TPT)

Just as you lay down certain rules and regulations for your children, God has laid down rules and regulations for you and He put them into permanent form—His Word. The next time the devil tries to steal your health, wealth, or your happiness, you can scream at the top of your lungs the same thing Mom said to the thief who tried to steal her car.

Start today and say,

"Devil, get your hands off of my life!
Who do you think you are? You can't steal my peace!
You can't steal what's mine!"

"FEAR NOT, FOR I AM WITH YOU"

Jehovah appeared to him on the night of his arrival. "I am the God of Abraham your father," he said. "Fear not, for I am with you and will bless you, and will give you so many descendants that they will become a great nation—because of my promise to Abraham, who obeyed me." (Genesis 26:24 TLB)

"Do not yield to fear, for I am always near. Never turn your gaze from me, for I am your faithful God. I will infuse you with my strength and help you in every situation. I will hold you firmly with my victorious right hand." (Isaiah 41:10 TPT)

In today's chaotic world, there's nothing greater to know than this. Your God is always nearby and ready to help. Thank You, Lord!

When you have any problem with fear or any other attack from the enemy, I suggest you write out all the Scriptures in this chapter. Post them on your bathroom mirror. Put a copy in your billfold to glance at when you are away from home. Memorize them so you can repeat them as often as you need them.

Use your authority. Remember, God is standing right next to you. You may not be able to "see" the devil or his demons, but they can "see" your Father, Jesus, and the Holy Spirit backing you up with power and full authority.

Whenever you are under attack, speak these words as loud as you can:

"Devil, you can't steal my peace!
My big brother, Jesus, will stomp on your head!"

4

FREEDOM FROM FEAR

Fear can kill you. Fear can literally stop you in your tracks. Physically, mentally, or spiritually, fear can paralyze you. You may not be free to even go around a corner. Fear can delay what God wants to do in and through your life. Learn to recognize the symptoms and know how to annihilate all forms of fear.

There can be dangerous life-changing episodes of fear; however, there is fear that does good things in your life also. What? Fear can be good? As you grow and develop from a small child, fear is a common feeling. How you handle it is the secret.

FEAR STARTS EARLY

A baby gets uncomfortable with a wet diaper or a hungry stomach. If mommy or daddy doesn't come when cries ring through the air, a baby can be afraid. Hurting a small child can damage or destroy a precious creation from God. Some small children are very daring and try all kinds of new things as they learn about life. It's fun to take those first steps, fall often, and get up to try again. The shy child is slow to try new things because they fell and got hurt the last time. Mommy or Daddy yelling at a child can also cause them to be very afraid.

ANNIHILATE FEAR

Trying new things can be very challenging as you develop and learn throughout life. Fear can pop up at any time. Many things can bring fear into your life.

The stove is hot and you can fear getting burned. Burns are very painful and can take a long time to heal. After you get burned, a form of fear will appear the next time you get near a stove or fire. Is this fear bad or good?

Life is filled with good and bad forms of fear. You have a choice. You learn what is dangerous and what is safe. Safe things don't cause fear. However, once you learn what is dangerous such as fire, you can either develop fear or respect.

What do I mean? Fire or heat can keep you warm in cold weather. It cooks your food. You can burn trash or unwanted things that are no longer useful. You learn and respect what fire can do including comfort, injury, or pain. Fire was discovered thousands of years ago and became very valuable to man. It was highly respected. Learn how to manage it.

If you handle fire carelessly, you can experience horrible burns that disfigure your body and leave lifelong reminders of your bad choices. Whether during an accident or carelessness, your experience will cause fear and negative memories of the trauma. These feelings of fear can last your entire life.

Instead, appreciate the value in fire and what it can do to improve your life. Enjoy watching the fire in the fireplace while staying a safe distance away.

DANGEROUS ACTIVITIES

Some people love to experience activities that are considered dangerous. The rush they feel is called exhilaration, and they may repeat it many times over. What are they doing? Skydiving out of a plane, bungee jumping off a thousand-foot-high bridge, hang-gliding, climbing a mountain or diving from a rocky cliff, or approaching a wild animal (such as a lion, alligator, wolf, or bear) or an approaching hurricane, tsunami, or hurricane.

Policemen, firemen, and servicemen and women certainly face fear when they are deployed into areas of fighting and warfare. What about racing cars, motorcycles, or four-wheelers? Washing windows on tall skyscrapers or walking around on girders while building the skyscrapers? Have you ever watched Nick Wallenda walk the highwire across Niagara Falls?

Many sports activities have a dangerous component to them such as skiing, football, basketball, and hockey. Have you ever watched *American Ninja Warrior*? Those participants have to be fearless to face such challenges. These activities are considered fun by many; however, others don't even want to watch.

ABUSE

All forms of abuse can easily develop negative and damaging fear. Physical, mental, and psychological abusive behaviors and memories can be extremely negative and damaging. Child abuse, spousal abuse, and elder abuse are but a few of the areas that make life miserable and full of fear.

Facing an illness, a surgical procedure, or dental work can cause the problem. Fear of the outcome or post-operative discomfort can cause many sleepless nights. Obviously, if the doctor gives you a negative report, fear enters your world. It's up to you to refuse that fear. I can't do it. Your pastor can't do it. You need to reject the fear and the thoughts that go along with that attack.

FEAR OF LACK

You can have a fear of lack. That includes lost finances, no job, no attention, no love, no house, no place to stay, no needed medicine,

ANNIHILATE FEAR

and no food to eat. The homeless, hungry, and needy are always with us. They may be sleeping under a bridge or begging for a handout. They fear each morning there will be no food. They fear each night trying to sleep on the ground or in a dark corner.

Several years ago, I was trying to figure out what in the world I was going to do. I was faced with the opportunity for fear and fear of lack to enter my life. The total of my tithe and house payment was more than I brought home from my secular job. I still had car payments and three girls in college, not to mention the house utility bills to pay.

The spirit of fear did come knocking on the door. I could have welcomed that spirit to come in and destroy my immune system. The increased stress could cause problems with my digestive system. All that fear could have prevented me from going to work, my only source of income.

The more I thought about it, the more I talked about it. "God, I don't know how You're going to do it. But you know what? That's not my responsibility. My responsibility is to do what You told me to do. I will be obedient in my tithe. I will be obedient in my offerings. I'm not going to worry or fear. If you take care of those little bitty birds outside, You're going to take care of me inside."

> "Look at the birds! They don't worry about what to eat—they don't need to sow or reap or store up food—for your heavenly Father feeds them. And you are far more valuable to him than they are." (Matthew 6:26 TLB)

> "Consider the ravens, for they neither sow nor reap, which have neither storehouse nor barn; and God feeds them. Of how much more value are you than the birds?" (Luke 12:24)

Because of my faith in my heavenly Father, I refused to allow fear to stay in my life. I cast out all fear. I cried out to God, "You're going to supply all of my needs according to Your riches and glory by Christ Jesus."

FEAR OF MINISTRY

> Are any of you sick? You should call for the elders of the church to come and pray over you, anointing you with oil in the name of the Lord. Such a prayer offered in faith will heal the sick, and the Lord will make you well. And if you have committed any sins, you will be forgiven. (James 5:14–15 NLT)

People you encounter may be afraid of prayer. They don't believe it will work for them. Showing love, compassion, and sincerity can calm their concerns. Offer to pray for whatever they need. They might have even been hurt by a church or other Christians.

Don't be afraid to offer to help anyone anywhere. Just be obedient and lay hands on the sick as you pray. When you get rid of your fear, you will minister to other people and see them healed. Enjoy watching sick people get well. Watching God work is really awesome. Praise God. Your job is to pray; God does the rest.

FEAR OF EXPECTATIONS

Children can be afraid of their parents, which then transfers to fear of other people in authority, such as teachers, ministers, or employers. Disappointment, unwarranted punishment, and failure can isolate and keep people from living a normal life. They may ignore or choose to stay away from other people who have never hurt them.

Many also have a fear of not meeting somebody's expectations. For example, your boss calls you in to his office. Immediately, you think, *What did I do?* He smiles and says, "I just wanted to tell you, you are doing a great job."

Maybe you get called into the principal's office. You just made the honor roll, but you think you're getting kicked out of school for three days. This is a very unhealthy but natural fear. People have a fear of going to their boss, talking to their boss, or talking to their dad or mom.

Parents expect children to excel at their studies and extracurricular activities. Unrealistic expectations can be damaging to the child, friend, or spouse.

Appreciate what each person is capable of, not your expectations. Encourage, help and love other people. Everyone is created as an individual, unique person by Father God. Don't ever walk in unrealistic expectations of yourself or of others.

IN THE NAME OF JESUS

People of all ages need to know Jesus and then they can say, "In the name of Jesus, I curse the spirit of fear. I curse the spirit of trauma!" No one needs to live in such fear. As soon as you recognize the symptoms of fear, take care of it immediately. Don't let it brew, multiply, or grow. Get rid of it!

Some people have a fear of turning into their parents. My mom was phenomenal. She loved Jesus with all her being and shared Jesus with everyone she met. She lived to be ninety-three. Even so, I don't want to be just like my mom. I don't want to be her. Obviously, I have a lot of similar characteristics, and there are a few characteristics that I work really hard not to have. I have no fear of being like my mom; however, I want to be who God wants me to be.

Keep your eyes on Jesus. Be the person God designed you to be. Don't be afraid of learning from your parents, but endeavor to become like your heavenly Father. Never fear what He has for your destiny. He loves you and will only do good things for you.

When I got the revelation so many years ago, I realized I was being attacked by the spirit of fear. Once I dealt with it, I never had that problem again.

Don't let that ugly, paralyzing spirit of fear enter any area of your life.

What is the difference between fear and the spirit of fear? As I have explained, fear can develop from many aspects of life. Once you learn to manage your negative feelings, basic fear can be a thing of the past. However, if you have developed or are plagued by the spirit of fear, this attack is from the enemy to destroy you. His victims feel fear frequently and may be very shy and won't take a risk to do anything new or different.

CHALLENGING SITUATIONS

Several years ago, my daughter Melody had many opportunities to deal with the spirit of fear personally. She hadn't been plagued with it overall; however, one thing after another happened over a period of several weeks, which could easily have become a serious problem.

She had seen many people who had experienced fear of flying and even driving a car. Her job required her to fly several times a week as well as drive to and from work. She didn't want fear to enter regarding either of these situations.

Realistically, very few have the option to avoid traveling by car. Walking long distances is not an option either. Our world has expanded so much, and transportation is required to get to a service, to work, to the airport or hotels. You have to learn how to deal with it.

She prayed, "Father, show me the good. What's the outcome that you have in mind? How are You going to turn this around?"

Just from seeing other people struggle with the spirit of fear and their inability to overcome was the beginning of a teaching series I gave on freedom from fear. The spirit of fear is the strongman behind depression, anxiety, and most mental illness. If you want a more in-depth study, read my book *Freedom Beyond Comprehension*.

You need His strength and confidence to do what God has called you to do without being hindered by fear.

Just because you have seen people burdened down by debt, working two or three jobs, becoming homeless, having cars being repossessed or a drug habit, doesn't mean you should expect to fall into that same position trapped by fear. Get rid of the mindset that God can't move beyond what your parents did or the platform that your parents established for you. Their generational curses or issues are not going to keep you from doing what God has called you to do. Get rid of fear.

Have you ever struggled with the spirit of fear? Are you trying to overcome the spirit of fear? Most people have experienced fear of some sort during their lifetime. Circumstances can come up quite often that challenge you on a day-to-day basis.

So many within the body of Christ are wrapped up in fear, depression, worry, and anxiety because they don't know what's happening next. You don't have to be in control of everything 24/7. That's God's job. Just find a little bit of faith in Him and relax. Speak encouragement and light to get rid of the darkness of fear.

Melody developed symptoms of an upper respiratory infection. The doctor called it an allergy, but she ended up with a double ear infection which resulted in temporary deafness. She was so sick, she couldn't leave her room for weeks. At twenty-five years of age, she felt fear and depression coming in. She was way too young to lose her hearing. She was feeling helpless.

People could have a confidential conversation nearby because she could not hear them or read lips. The doctor was telling her she would just have to wait for the symptoms to resolve on their own. She was not happy.

She called out to God, "God, I can't do this. There's no way I can do what you've called me to do if I can't hear. So, God, how are you going to override this?" She could see what was going on, but did not understand. She was very frustrated because she could not even drive her car without hearing.

Think for a minute, how would you handle your life if you couldn't hear? No phone calls, no TV, no radio, no talking with your loved ones. Writing notes would be your only means of communication. Doesn't sound like fun, does it?

One evening after dealing with the loss of hearing for over three weeks, she coughed and literally felt the pressure change in her ears. She picked up her phone and could hear!

She was so happy to have her health restored and get back to normal activities. Even now, if she feels anything a bit abnormal, she quickly says, "God, I thank You that this is not going to affect my ears. God, I thank You that I will never be that sick ever again. Father, I thank You." And she praises Him in the middle of her symptoms, claiming that she will never experience anything like that again.

When Melody originally moved to Kingwood, Texas, she had bought a new car. Just as she was pulling out of the neighborhood one day, a guy who didn't know the light was there ran over the front end of her car. Then he hit a second, third, fourth, and fifth car. She saw his big Bronco hit one car after the other while sliding on two wheels. It seemed like an action scene in a movie.

Her hands clamped down on the steering wheel. She had no idea what to do and couldn't really see what was happening with the other vehicles and drivers. She even forgot her dog was in the backseat. During the crash, the dog got stuck in between the back and front seats. Melody knew she had to get her precious friend out of the car. She panicked and called me.

I could hear the hysteria in her voice as she said, "I'm right outside your neighborhood. I just need you to come and get me."

I asked, "Where are you?"

She replied, "I'm right here! Do you not understand? Just follow the sound of panic. You can find me there! Use your mom GPS on me and find me. I'm two minutes from your house. I haven't even made it out of the neighborhood."

Since her car was totaled, she had to ride with a friend to school the next day. She doesn't like riding with anyone else driving, and when she got into that car, fear overwhelmed her. She was scared about getting into a car within twenty-four hours of the car crash. Just as plain as day, she envisioned the car accident happening again. She nearly passed out from fear to see it in her mind again and again.

You can open up the spirit of fear after experiencing something so traumatic and then reliving it again and again. Many people live the trauma once and then choose to relive it every single day because they don't deal with the trauma. Repetition makes them relive it every single day.

You have a choice. You can say, "I can just push through and not deal with it. I can just push it down." Instead, please deal with it so you don't relive it. Address the issue of the trauma and fear so you won't have to relive it again and again and again.

Does anybody know the definition for the word fear? It's

actually a pretty interesting definition. Wikipedia explains it this way: "Fear is an emotion induced by perceived danger or threat, which causes physiological changes and ultimately behavioral changes, such as fleeing, hiding, or freezing from perceived traumatic events. Fear in human beings may occur in response to a certain stimulus occurring in the present, or in anticipation or expectation of a future threat perceived as a risk to oneself. The fear response arises from the perception of danger leading to confrontation with or escape from/avoiding the threat (also known as the fight-or-flight response), which in extreme cases of fear (horror and terror) can be a freeze response or paralysis."

In short, fear is the ability to recognize danger and cause a fight-or-flight response, a protective body response to fight or run away. Every time you are afraid or deal with the spirit of fear, adrenaline is released throughout your body to give you the necessary strength to defend yourself or run away from danger.

The spirit of fear can be dangerous if you're dealing with it on a regular basis. With a frequent release of adrenaline, your body can develop adrenal failure and burnout.

Wisdom is required when dealing with the spirit of fear. Because fear is a protective measure, you need to recognize when you are supposed to face it and fight it. Wisdom will also tell you when you avoid or leave the situation that is causing fear. In other words, run away from it.

DAVID'S EXAMPLE

Read the story of David fighting Goliath in 1 Samuel 17. David could have easily run the other direction to avoid a confrontation with the giant Goliath. He could have collapsed in fear. At times, fear can be a stimulus to stand up and face the enemy because you know God is right there with you to help where you are lacking.

ANNIHILATE FEAR

David knew God was his strength and would take care of him despite all the negative remarks from his brothers and the giant.

When you fight a battle, you may have people telling you that you are not able, not smart enough, or not strong enough. Find people who will give you their blessing and say, "Go for it and let the Lord be with you."

I won't give up and admit that fear beat me. I will not cower in a corner. I will overcome the circumstances that tried to rise up against me. Because He is still the living God and my Father.

Stand strong in the face of a financial bear or some type of a lion at work. Know that you are going to be the overcomer because you can tie it back to Scripture where people who looked like underdogs totally succeeded.

Walk in confidence when facing a battle of fear. Rebuke the spirit of fear as well as all anxiety, depression, co-dependency, bitterness, resentment, and abuse.

Overcoming the spirit of fear is not ignoring wisdom. It's recognizing the fact that God is right there with you. David knew that God would protect him, even in this battle. He faced the fear with confidence that God was going to deliver him out of the hand of the Philistines. The truth of who God is stood firmer than Goliath ever could.

OBEY HIS DIRECTION

When you're walking with Him, you're walking in the firm footsteps of what He has for you. When you're facing all that you have to face, you will be the overcomer no matter what because God is with you.

Pursuing what God has for you can also be a scary thing. It can open up the door for fear; however, if you're doing what God has called you to do, it's not going to be scary. You're going to be totally assured of everything that you're doing. If you aren't a bit nervous about God's plan for your life, you don't need His help. He will challenge you, but He designed you and already planned your destiny.

When you start working in ministry, fear can try to come in. What if they get offended because they don't like that you're a believer? Or what if you lose a friend because they don't like that you're a Christian? Or if they don't like your post online that you're a believer?

How does fear get in? The spirit of fear is sneaky. It watches where you open a door. Fear literally stays more aware than you are. It knows how to get its foot in the door. I'm talking about the situation with the car accident or planes having really bad turbulence or aborting a flight due to a mechanical issue. "God, I thank You that this plane is going to make it home without a problem, and without some alarm or some signal going off up there with the captain."

What could open the door for you? Maybe you don't fly very often. Sometimes when you see situations where friends and family go through a hard time or a sickness or a disease or divorce, you can get a "what if that happens to me" mentality. You can look at the situation and wonder what to do, how to fix it, or how to make things better. Avoid entertaining those thoughts. Ask God!

There was a lady who lived in the Midland-Odessa area of Texas, and her family had a history of breast cancer. She had gone to the doctor and was diagnosed with the dreaded disease. She came to a service, got prayed for, and was totally healed and verified by the doctors. In fear of the breast cancer coming back, she had a double mastectomy and went through all the chemo and radiation treatments. She lost her hair and her health because she was terrified of the cancer returning. She died of a heart attack because of the worry, stress, and fear.

Fear is a cage that can kill your dreams and drown your hopes. It needs to be addressed within the body of Christ, so that we don't allow it to enter our lives.

> "For I know the plans I have for you," says the Lord.
> "They are plans for good and not for disaster, to give you a future and a hope." (Jeremiah 29:11 NLT)

PANDEMIC

If you surround God's plan with a cage of fear, you will never step into or fulfill His purpose for your life. Take each step within God's plan for your destiny.

Another door that can open you up to fear is purposely watching scary things. People actually spend good money to get scared. Why would you choose scary movies, haunted houses, or staying in a hotel in a bad neighborhood? Everyday life can offer that little moment for fear to sneak in. It can start innocently enough and then multiply until you are paralyzed. You can't leave the house. You don't want to drive anywhere. You don't want to fly anywhere.

Unfortunately, fear multiplied countless times during the pandemic of 2020 and following. Many have found they can do almost everything directly from home. With the internet, working from home became more common than ever. School for all ages became virtual (streamed online from the institution). Food from grocery stores and prepared meals from restaurants could be delivered to your doorstep. Wearing masks and social distancing were mandated.

Order whatever you want online so you don't have to get in

your car to go to the store. You don't need to get gas for your car for fear of getting mugged. Since you aren't driving much, your car doesn't need much gas. Isolation reigned. Listening to the negative news just added to the paralyzing fear.

The fear and the phobia that people live in is amazing. You can easily wonder how they survived to adulthood. Or, how they made it as long as they did because they deal with such fear. So, it's time for the body of Christ to get rid of fear.

5

FEAR TO FAITH

We ought to have this next verse underlined, scribbled on, marked with a marking pencil or something equally distinctive in our Bibles.

> But without faith it is impossible to please Him. (Hebrews 11:6)

It is impossible to please God if you don't have faith!

It is impossible to please God if you don't exercise your faith!

You cannot please God when you have doubt and unbelief in your life. Without faith, it is totally, completely 100 percent impossible to please God. The Word explains:

> For he that cometh to God must believe that He is, and the He is a rewarder of them that diligently seek Him. (Hebrews 11:6)

First of all, you've got to believe that He *is*. How do you discover that He *is*? Through reading the Word of God, you discover that God *is*. You have to believe that He is a *rewarder* of them that diligently seek Him.

The hungry people in the nations around the world need to

know and *believe* what the Word of God says. They can never please Him until they have faith. And they certainly don't have faith when they are starving to death and don't know anything about the only true God, the God who said, "I Am."

> If any of you lack wisdom, let him ask of God, that giveth to all men liberally, and upbraideth not; and it shall be given him. But let him ask in faith, nothing wavering. For he that wavereth is like a wave of the sea driven with the wind and tossed. For let not that man think that he shall receive any thing of the Lord. He is a double-minded man, unstable in all his ways.
> (James 1:5–8 KJV)

Don't you dare waver! If and when you do, His Word says that you are like a wave of the sea that is tossed and turned by the wind with no direction or purpose. A man who wavers between faith and doubt and unbelief will not receive a thing! Verse 8 says, "A double-minded man is unstable in all his ways."

Sometimes we forget what that really means. You cannot come to church on Sunday morning and say, "Jesus is Lord," and then walk out and live the direct opposite for the rest of the week. God is real at all times. If you believe God is real, then don't you dare go around wavering all week long, saying, "God doesn't answer my prayers. The devil has got more power than God has, and nothing good ever seems to happen to me."

I want *everything* that God has for me. I will not speak words of unbelief and doubt!

Praise God that He is so plain and simple in His directions to us. Does He tell us to continue in the devil's bible? No, He certainly does not, but He plainly says to continue in His Word!

I remember when the spirit of fear came on me. I was about

eight years old. My older brother had done something to make our mother very mad. My mother was about five foot seven. My brother at that time was about six foot three. She looked up at him and said, "No matter how old you are or how big, you will never be too big for me to slap." She slapped him and knocked him to the ground.

At that moment, I felt fear enter me. I knew I would never ever do anything to make her mad. I determined I would never make anyone else mad either. Keep in mind that this was before my mom got saved. After witnessing that incident, I had a greater respect for my mother and the power she had. Not only fear of her but fear of other people also.

My biological father was a very violent man. He had tried to kill my mom while she was pregnant with me. He also beat her regularly until she left him. I was afraid of him beating me as well as possibly getting physically disciplined from my mother. These incidents brought on that spirit of fear within me.

When I got married in 1974, I would lay in bed and shake uncontrollably. My husband would ask, "What is wrong with you?" There was nothing within him that would cause him to hurt me. But I could not stop shaking.

I had no idea what to do. I sought help from a lady minister who was a very good friend. I had to learn how to get rid of this torment. I remember getting prayer and getting healed.

Every once in a while, fear still raises its ugly head and whispers in my ear. I have had to learn to fight it and chase it away. I am so happy today to be able to say, "I am totally free." It has been amazing to get free from fear. God protects me from any attacks from the spirit of fear.

So many Christians have been attacked by fear. A friend had an encounter with the Lord in 2020. In a dream, the spirit of fear came in and told him to tell the body of Christ, "Thank you for feeding me!"

Do you understand? Each time you allow the enemy to upset you with his lies, you are feeding him and giving him more ammunition to continue his attacks. He becomes stronger and stronger in your life. It is like ignoring God and His protection and choosing to listen and believe the enemy instead.

God is always there with peace and love in His hand waiting for you to reach out and accept all the good things He has to offer. It has been amazing to live free in God's presence. I am no longer afraid of anything—man, lack, etc.

I want you to get free and healed from the spirit of fear also. Choose God. Pray: "Father, in the name of Jesus, I curse any kind of stress, trauma, and spirit of fear as well as where the spirit of fear entered. Father, I thank You for removing all the trauma regarding that situation. Father, keep me protected from the attacks of the enemy. Give me revelation so I can and will recognize any attack so I can stand strong in You and Your Word. In Jesus' name. Amen."

TRUTH

> "If ye continue in my word, then are ye my disciples; indeed, and ye shall know the truth, and the truth shall make you free." (John 8:31–32 KJV)

Once you know the truth, the truth is going to make you absolutely, totally, and completely free. That is why the devil hates it when you really understand the truth, when you know what the truth says, and when you have hidden the Word so deep in your heart that the devil can't snatch it away from you. God wants you to plant His Word so deeply that the devil can't steal it.

If you know the story of Shadrach, Meshach, and Abednego,

you remember they were told to worship a god that they didn't believe in or be put to death. Even with the threat of death, these three young men still stood and refused to obey those orders. They knew that the living God would take care of them.

> "Whoever does not fall down and worship will immediately be thrown into a blazing furnace. Shadrach, Meshach and Abednego—who pay no attention to you, Your Majesty. They neither serve your gods nor worship the image of gold you have set up."

Shadrach, Meshach and Abednego were told:

> "If you don't obey, what God can save you from my hand? What God can rescue you from my hand physically hurting you?" Shadrach, Meshach and Abednego replied to him, "King Nebuchadnezzar, we do not need to defend ourselves before you in this matter. If we are thrown into the blazing furnace, the God we serve is able to deliver us from it, and he will deliver us from Your Majesty's hand. But even if he does not, we want you to know, Your Majesty, that we will not serve your gods or worship the image of gold you have set up." (Daniel 3:6, 12, 15–16 NIV)

The three men were saying, "With everything in me, I know that God's going to deliver us, but even if He doesn't, we are not going to bow down or serve another god."

Nebuchadnezzar got so mad that he had the furnace turned up seven times higher than normal.

> The king's command was so urgent and the furnace so hot that the flames of the fire killed the soldiers who took up Shadrach, Meshach and Abednego. (Daniel 3:22 NIV)

ANNIHILATE FEAR

The oven was so hot, the king's soldiers who didn't even get thrown into it were burned. "And these three men, firmly tied, fell into the blazing furnace" (v. 23 NIV) while King Nebuchadnezzar and his entourage stood there watching. "[The King] said, 'Look! I see four men walking around in the fire, unbound and unharmed, and the fourth looks like a son of the gods'" (v. 25). He recognized a fourth person in the blazing fire with the three young men, and none of them were hurt. None of them were bound.

> Nebuchadnezzar then approached the opening of the blazing furnace and shouted, "Shadrach, Meshach and Abednego, servants of the Most High God, come out! Come here!" So Shadrach, Meshach and Abednego came out of the fire, and the satraps, prefects, governors and royal advisers crowded around them. They saw that the fire had not harmed their bodies, nor was a hair of their heads singed; their robes were not scorched, and there was no smell of fire on them. (v. 26)

That's how you overcome fear. You can face whatever it is that's against you, and you overcome it. You will still come out smelling good versus smelling like the situation you were just in.

> Then Nebuchadnezzar said, "Praise be to the God of Shadrach, Meshach and Abednego, who has sent his angel and rescued his servants! They trusted in him and defied the king's command and were willing to give up their lives rather than serve or worship any god except their own God. Therefore I decree that the people of any nation or language who say anything against the God of Shadrach, Meshach and Abednego be cut into pieces and their houses be turned into

piles of rubble, for no other god can save in this way." (v. 28–29 NIV)

That is part of our victory. No other god can save in this way. Nothing else can save you from what's going on. Nothing else can put up a barrier of protection around you or situations that you're facing. It is God and God alone who will keep you safe. It is Him and Him alone Who provides and saves in this way.

In China, if you've not been threatened because you are a believer, they don't even take you seriously. They want you to live in such a way that it doesn't matter what else is going on; you will serve the one true God and don't care if you have to lay your life down for your beliefs. That's the bar that they raise for other believers.

Are you willing to give up everything, all that you know and have, and your life, to say that God is real and true? Let me ask you, if you were being tortured and the only way to stop your physical body from being tortured was to say you didn't believe in God, would you do it?

Yes, I know this is totally one of those left-field questions. What would you do? People used to talk about what would happen if or when Christianity was outlawed. Someone would put a gun to your head and ask, "Do you believe?" If you deny your faith in Christ, they let you live. If you stand on your faith and say, "Yes," they will kill you. Boom, you're dead and in heaven.

What if they torture you? You can feel that pain until they kill you. Everything within me would say, "Yes, I believe." Because everything I've stood for, everything I've lived for has been that God is real. The living God is my source of strength and my source of life. If I couldn't admit my faith, I don't know how I'd be able to live after that.

Okay. What if they were torturing one of your loved ones

and you had to watch? I could probably handle it myself, but to endure watching my friends and family would be difficult. Would I be able to do that and say that God is still real? Yes, while I prayed for God's deliverance from everything happening.

That's the belief, that's the strength, that's the source that you have to have to know that beyond everything, you believe in God and profess that God is the living God. Not looking at the consequences or reality of the fear that you face, know that God will save you.

Overcome the spirit of fear by the word of your testimony. Stop entertaining your fear with the what-if thoughts. Look at things and say, "You know what, instead of imagining what's going on or happening, I'm going to find out God's reality and not ignore His truth."

Face the truth. Accept the reality of the situation. Deal with the spirit of fear. Deal with the "I don't know what's going to happen" through prayer and petition: "God, this is a difficult situation I am facing. I really don't know what to do. You know the outcome. You know the path I should take and the words I should say. Guide me, please. In Jesus' holy name. Amen."

Seek godly counsel and godly wisdom when you're facing a choice and don't know the next step to take. Your responsibility as a believer is to find other people who can help you.

Thank God that endless Christian teachers and preachers are available online. You can listen to His Word 24/7. Beautiful uplifting, encouraging music can roll through your home and surround you with His love. Listen to Him, not the news.

The biggest key is facing your fear. If you don't face fear, it will always have power over you. Giving in to fear will always cut your potential short. Choose to stand on the knowledge and the fact that God has got your back in all situations.

For God has not given us a spirit of fear, but of power and of love and of a sound mind. (2 Timothy 1:7)

God did not give us the spirit of fear, so it's not ours to hold on to. Do not claim it as yours. It may appear in passing, but that is all. Get rid of it.

JESUS WALKS ON WATER

Immediately after this, Jesus insisted that his disciples get back into the boat and cross to the other side of the lake, while he sent the people home. After sending them home, he went up into the hills by himself to pray. Night fell while he was there alone. Meanwhile, the disciples were in trouble far away from land, for a strong wind had risen, and they were fighting heavy waves.

About three o'clock in the morning Jesus came toward them, walking on the water. When the disciples saw him walking on the water, they were terrified. In their fear, they cried out, "It's a ghost!" But Jesus spoke to them at once. "Don't be afraid," he said. "Take courage. I am here!" Then Peter called to him, "Lord, if it's really you, tell me to come to you, walking on the water." "Yes, come," Jesus said.

So Peter went over the side of the boat and walked on the water toward Jesus. But when he saw the strong wind and the waves, he was terrified and began to sink. "Save me, Lord!" he shouted. Jesus immediately reached out and grabbed him. "You have so little faith," Jesus said. "Why did you doubt me?"

When they climbed back into the boat, the wind stopped. Then the disciples worshiped him. "You really are the Son of God!" they exclaimed. (Matthew 14:22–33 NLT)

Those disciples faced the scariest storm that's ever mentioned in the Bible. And where were they? Right in the middle of obedience to what Jesus told them to do. They had just seen Jesus feeding the five thousand. Now he calmed the storm and they believed. Their faith exploded to a new level. Jesus brought peace to the storm.

After reading about this storm, I want to challenge you. Take every thought captive. When fear comes in at the beginning of a thought or circumstance that you're facing, you may think, *This could kill me.* Before you even say aloud or think, *This could overtake me,* take that thought captive the way that the Word says to. Don't look for doors of opportunity for fear to come in. Don't unnecessarily go down a dark alley or walk into dangerous situations.

Bravery is not looking for a fearful situation, bravery is being strong when you have to be. Knowing God is walking with me will always assure me that I can draw on His wisdom.

Another good key for you. Don't play the what-if mind game. What if we lose it all? What if he gets laid off? What if they take our house? What if they take our car? Losing things can be an inconvenience. But God is still in control.

Shadrach, Meshach, and Abednego were willing to let go of everything to do what God had called them to do and to stand faithful to God. Focus on what God has called you to do and walk in obedience. His rod and His staff are there comforting you, regardless of what you're facing (see Psalm 23:4).

Put your hand over your heart and pray, "Father, in the name of Jesus, I curse the spirit of trauma and I command it to go. I curse the spirit of fear and timidity and command it to go in

Jesus' name. I speak peace and health and wholeness. I curse any voice or thought in each person's mind and heart that is not of you. And in Jesus' name, I not only tell it to be silent, but to be gone. In Jesus' name. Father, I thank You and give You glory for the fact that I can walk in freedom from fear. I can walk knowing that You're directing every single step that I have to take. Father, I thank You that Your Word declares that You have a plan and a purpose for me. I choose to live a life free from fear. In Jesus' name. Hallelujah! Amen."

Repeat that prayer whenever you need to. Call out to Jesus. He will rebuke the storm raging around you. He helps you walk on the water in peace. Remember these verses:

> "You whom I have taken from the ends of the earth, and called from its farthest regions, and said to you, You are My servant, I have chosen you and have not cast you away: Fear not, for I am with you; be not dismayed, for I am your God. I will strengthen you, yes, I will help you, I will uphold you with My righteous right hand." (Isaiah 41:9–11)

> "You must not fear them, for the Lord your God Himself fights for you." (Deuteronomy 3:22)

> "Be strong and of good courage, do not fear nor be afraid of them; for the Lord your God, He is the One who goes with you. He will not leave you nor forsake you." (Deuteronomy 31:6)

> So he answered, "Do not fear, for those who are with us are more than those who are with them." (2 Kings 6:16)

> Though an army may encamp against me, My heart

ANNIHILATE FEAR

shall not fear; though war may rise against me, In this I will be confident. (Psalm 27:3)

In God (I will praise His word), In God I have put my trust; I will not fear. What can flesh do to me? (Psalm 56:4)

The Lord is on my side; I will not fear. What can man do to me? (Psalm 118:6)

In righteousness you shall be established; You shall be far from oppression, for you shall not fear; And from terror, for it shall not come near you. (Isaiah 54:14)

Fear not, O land; be glad and rejoice, for the Lord has done marvelous things! (Joel 2:21)

"Do not fear, little flock, for it is your Father's good pleasure to give you the kingdom." (Luke 12:32)

So we may boldly say: "The Lord is my helper; I will not fear. What can man do to me?" (Hebrews 13:6)

Through all these verses, God is certainly telling you to stand strong, rebuke fear, and believe in His protection and love. Choose God!

6
DEVELOP YOUR FAITH

Is faith the opposite of fear? Not exactly. However, using your faith will help you have victory over fear. What do I mean? Your faith is a weapon in your arsenal of weapons to fight the enemy. Just like the armor of God, you need to put on your faith every day. Be ready to repel the attack of the enemy, especially the spirit of fear.

For instance, if you are afraid or have a spirit of fear related to your finances, as a child of God, you will depend on God to provide what you need. In other words, God will take care of your fear. The name of Jesus will defeat any spirit of fear that tries to attach itself to you.

Many things you face every day have the potential of bringing fear into your life. What are you going to do about that? Before you even get out of bed in the morning, you can simply ask God for His protection and provision for the day. You need His wisdom and guidance for everything you do. Ask for it. After all, you are one of His children.

Your faith will activate God and His angels to guide your steps and lead you. Open your eyes and listen carefully to His words. His Holy Spirit is your Guide, your Comforter, your Wise Counsel.

Faith in His Word is so important. Faith in Him is likewise.

Many use the word *faith* rather carelessly about needless things. But God considers it a valuable and very necessary part of the Christian life. Let's talk about faith. You and I both need it every day we live.

Webster's Dictionary is prolific in many descriptions of words, but where faith is concerned, he is extremely simple but beautiful. He merely says it is "unquestioning belief in God… complete trust, confidence, or reliance; as children usually have faith in their parents."

Faith is "unquestioning belief" in who God is, in what He does, and what He says. How can you know what God has to say? Many ways, but probably the best way to hear His voice is to read what His Word says.

In the beginning of my mom's Christian life, someone told her there were more than seventy thousand promises in the Word of God. I remember her saying, "Oh, God, let me live long enough to claim each and every one of those promises for myself!" She wanted everything God had. Her reasoning was: "How am I going to know what God has for me unless I read the Bible?" She was determined to sit down to read the entire Bible.

One morning God told her to read the book of Galatians. She opened it and zipped right down through the first six verses, thinking this was the "milk" of the Word, and started getting serious along about verse seven. In the stillness of her office, she heard the small, still voice of God, the voice that we so often miss because we're so busy with our own plans, or because we think God has to shout at us. He said, "Go back!"

She thought, *Whoops, I must have missed something there*, so she went back, and this is the way she read the first part of Galatians:

DEVELOP YOUR FAITH

"Paulanapostle—notfrommennorthroughman,butthroughJesus-ChristandGodtheFatherwhoraisedhimfromthedead!" She read it as fast as she could and went on to what she considered the "meat" of that chapter. Once again, she heard that small, still voice say, "Go back!"

She thought, *Maybe I read it a little too fast.* She read it a little slower, saying, "Paul, an apostle—not from men nor through man, but through Jesus Christ and God the Father, who raised him from the dead…" (Galatians 1:1 RSV). She said, "But God, I didn't know Paul. He died a few years before I was born."

Then God spoke the words that changed her life. He said, "I'm talking to YOU." In the twinkling of an eye, she realized that God had not only written the Bible for the scholars of old, but also for her in the middle of the twentieth century. She scratched out Brother Paul's name and wrote *Frances*. Suddenly, the Bible came alive to her because she realized that God was speaking to *her*!

During the years, I have done the same thing. God now speaks to me, Joan, with every verse in the Bible. If I need or want an answer from Him, the first place I look is in my Bible. I have several different versions on my bookshelf. Occasionally, I will look in more than one version to get a complete answer. I am so grateful that my God and Father left His Word for me to study so I know His will.

The minute you understand that almighty God is speaking to you personally through the pages of His Word, the quicker your faith will begin to rise also. God is speaking to you! Put your name throughout the Bible, and see what God has to say to you personally and then watch your faith meter begin to soar.

> In the beginning God created the heaven and the earth. (Genesis 1:1 KJV)

ANNIHILATE FEAR

Webster's Dictionary says that the word *create* means, "To originate; to bring into being from nothing; to cause to exist." There was nothing. From nothing, God created the universe. How did He create it?

The book of Hebrews gives us an important clue that can unlock the entire Bible to you in a totally new and different way.

> Faith empowers us to see that the universe was created and beautifully coordinated by the power of God's words! He spoke and the invisible realm gave birth to all that is seen. (Hebrews 11:3 TPT)

By the *Word* of God. Not by the hands of God. Not by the mind of God. Not by the feet of God. Not by the power of God, but by the *Word* of God.

> And God said, let there be light: and there was light. (Genesis 1:3 KJV)

> And God said, let there be a firmament in the midst of the waters, let it divide the waters from the waters… and it was so. (Genesis 1:6 KJV)

> And God said, Let the earth bring forth grass, the herb yielding seed, and the fruit tree yielding fruit after his kind, whose seed is in it-self, upon the earth and it was so. (Genesis 1:11 KJV)

> And God said, let us make man in our image, after our likeness: and let them have dominion over the fish of the sea, and over every creeping thing that creeps upon the earth. So, God created man in His own image, in the image of God created he him; male and female created he them. (Genesis 1:26 KJV)

Did you notice that every verse started with "God said"? Then it became and it was so. Whenever God speaks, whether it is in the Old Testament or the New Testament, it is God *speaking*.

God merely spoke, just as you and I speak. When He spoke, the world was formed. God made man in the likeness of Himself, a copy, an exact duplicate of Himself.

Man was fashioned after God, and God gave this man, Adam, dominion over all things, the fish of the sea, the fowls of the air, the animals walking on land, and every creeping thing that creeps upon the earth. This means Adam was in charge of everything that God made—*everything*!

Notice that God did not "speak" man into existence. God "created" man from the dust of the ground. Adam must have appeared to God as a doll appears to us with shape and form, but no life. I visualize God holding Adam gently in His arms cradling him like a baby. When God leaned down and breathed life into his nostrils, Adam became "a living soul."

When children are small, parents tell them many things. They hear the familiar loving voices and often know what parents mean by the tone of voice long before they understand the actual words. Children hear because an adult they trust speaks to them.

For a period of time, children believe every word spoken by their parents. Then they begin to grow up, and their minds expand. They believe they are smarter than their parents and try things for themselves.

Like little birds trying to fly, they try their wings. They discover when they don't follow their parent's advice, they flop to the ground. When they listen to instructions, and move correctly, they can fly short distances. Eventually, they soar.

The Word of God to Christians is the same as a mother or father speaking to their child. If we do what God tells us to do, we will face challenges but not experience unsurmountable problems which we can't overcome.

> Blessed be the Lord, who has given rest to His people Israel, according to all that He promised. There has not failed one word of all His good promise, which He promised through His servant Moses. (1 Kings 8:56)

God has never failed, and He will never fail. In addition, He will never lie about any situation.

> Then the Lord said to me, "You have seen well, for I am ready to perform My word." (Jeremiah 1:12)

> God is not a man, that He should lie, nor a son of man, that He should repent. Has He said, and will He not do? Or has He spoken, and will He not make it good? (Numbers 23:19)

There is no way that God can back down from the Word He has spoken. Every single sentence, every single word that is in the Word of God is exactly the same as if God sat down beside you and spoke His words into your ears.

> All scripture is given by inspiration of God, and is profitable for doctrine, for reproof, for correction, for instruction in righteousness" (2 Timothy 3:16)

We speak to our children to instruct them and correct them, for discipline, obedience. and training. God speaks to us through His Word to instruct and guide us. The Christian life is simple because all we have to do is two things:

1. Do what God tells us to do.
2. Stop doing what He tells us not to do.

DEVELOP YOUR FAITH

That's all there is to it and you've got it made!
And how do you do what God wants you to do?

> I consider your prophecies to be my greatest treasure, and I memorize them and write them on my heart to keep me from committing sin's treason against you. (Psalm 119:11 TPT)

> Forever, O Lord, thy word is settled in heaven. (Psalm 119:89 KJV)

Establish in your own mind that every single verse that is printed on the pages of the Bible is the actual spoken Word of God written down for you. Then your faith can begin that upward climb as you begin to memorize and hide His Word in your heart.

How do you increase your faith?

> Faith cometh by hearing, and hearing by the word of God. (Romans 10:17 KJV)

Read the Word of God, hear the Word of God, and understand the Word of God. How can you understand what He is telling you? By reading the Bible. The Bible is God's personal love letter to His children. If you seek God by reading, believing, and confessing His Word, every one of His promises is yours.

Faith and the promises of God work together. As you read the Word of God, your inner man will be quickened by the Holy Spirit as His promises begin to speak to you. Before long, you will begin to "experiment" with the Word of God. Realize that all the promises of God have a condition to them. You do your part and God will do His part. Believe enough for one promise from God, and you will be amazed at what God will do.

I remember the first time I ever saw an arm grow out. I didn't know if I believed it or not. The second time, I saw this supernatural phenomenon of God with my own eyes, I no longer doubted. A lady had an arm that was about three inches shorter than the other. I was sitting on the stage about two feet from her. My faith began to rise as I saw God's promise and His Word come together in healing her.

Since God is no respecter of persons, Dad and Mom decided that God's miracle power could do the same thing for the people in their services. Everyone was instructed to measure their arms. There seems to always be at least one person with arms of unequal lengths. They prayed for each person individually and saw God's miracle with their own eyes!

God honored His Word which says that those who believe "shall lay hands on the sick, and they shall recover" (Mark 16:18 KJV). God said it. It became. It was so. Every arm grew out!

With every healing, their faith rose! Why? Because Mom and Dad exercised their faith. The same thing happened to me as I watched these miracles. Soon, I was following my parents' example. I saw the same miracles.

> Thus also faith by itself, if it does not have works, is dead. (James 2:17)

Faith cannot grow unless it is exercised! People who do not exercise a muscle lose function of that muscle. For instance, if a child is left in a bed without any activity, their muscles will atrophy. They will not develop strength, balance, or walking ability. Any muscle in your body which is not used will get weak, and the same is true of your faith.

Years ago, a friend of mine met foster parents who were taking care of a twelve-year-old girl. The birth parents had left the child in a small closet most of her life. The child couldn't walk or talk and was still in diapers. She crawled and scooted around on the floor like a monkey and ate food off the floor with her fingers. She had been sorely neglected. Her birth parents had taught her nothing. Her muscles were poorly developed from the lack of normal healthy exercise.

What was even sadder, she would not raise her head to look at anyone. She stared at the floor all the time. One cannot even imagine the abuse she had endured to survive. Thank God, she was found and placed in a Christian home where she could start living.

The more you use your faith, the more it will grow. The less you use it, the weaker it will become. Every time I call for those who need healing, my faith grows stronger because I see God do miracles nearly every day.

After Mom and Dad first saw just one arm grow, they wondered if God could lengthen more than one person's arm at a time. They exercised their baby faith and prayed that God would heal an entire audience at one time, and He did!

Their faith continued to rise until they saw God heal the short arms of entire audiences in every seminar. They used this particular kind of faith over and over, and God never failed! I watched and learned. Then I started doing the same thing. My faith grew, and I have never stopped exercising my faith "muscle."

Imagine Jesus sitting down in your living room and telling you:

> "Again I say unto you, That if two of you shall agree on earth as touching anything that they shall ask, it shall be done for them of my Father which is in heaven. For where two or three are gathered together in my name, there am I in the midst of them." (Matthew 18:19–20 KJV)

ANNIHILATE FEAR

Faith will come easily if you really believe that it is Jesus talking just to you, and not just some words that someone printed on paper. The Old and New Testaments are truths from both God and Jesus as They speak to you. Imagine you could reach out and touch them right now.

Your faith can never accept those Scriptures until you reach out and exercise it. Ask God for something which you know is in line with His will, get someone to agree with you, pray for it, claim His promise, and see what happens.

When Mom first became a Christian, she became a fanatic for the Word of God. She would stay up until two or three o'clock in the morning reading, and reading, and reading, and *reading* the Word of God. She was like a huge sponge that just couldn't get enough of His living water.

She read the New Testament numerous times the first few months. As she read some of those favorite passages, her spirit-man stirred inside of her. She determined to test God. She said, "I believe I'll do it. God's Word says it will happen, so I'm going to try it!"

One verse that really spoke to her was in Matthew.

> "And all things, whatsoever ye shall ask in prayer, believing, ye shall receive." (Matthew 21:22 KJV)

Her faith rose up. "All I have to do is believe." And so, she believed. It was as simple as that.

The pastor who led her to the Lord once told her, "God answers the dumbest prayers when they are spoken in faith believing." He said this because Mom had asked God to transport a whipped-cream cherry pie from Miami to Columbus, Ohio, to strengthen the bonds of Christian love. She very simply believed that God would do it—and He did it!

DEVELOP YOUR FAITH

The same pastor gave her the wisest advice she was ever given. Right after she was saved at age forty-nine, he said to her, "Frances, at your age, you'll never make it—unless you come with the faith of a little child, just believing."

Mom became a Christian with the simple faith of a little child. She never changed. She always believed all things are possible with God. Watching Mom take each baby step built my faith. I knew if God could change my mom, He had to be real. That powerful witness my mom showed me each day made me want to experience the same love from Father God.

You say you don't have enough faith to try anything? Oh, yes, you do. We all have faith in something! Let me show you some examples where you have tremendous faith. For instance, when I need to go to the store, I get in my car, put the key in the ignition, start the car's engine, and drive out of the driveway.

I have absolute faith in my ability to drive a car. I've driven for many years. Why do I have faith in driving a car? Because I do it all the time. Because I exercised my faith driving the first time, I had more faith the second time. I didn't get to be a good driver in two or three lessons. But eventually I became an excellent driver. Today, it doesn't even take faith to drive my car. It's automatic because I've done it so many times.

Your faith in God can become the same way. Listen to CDs, talk to God, memorize Scripture, and pray. Soon you won't even think about needing faith. You will sincerely believe God's Word and His promises.

I also have tremendous faith in my household appliances. When I put my dirty clothes into the washer, add the soap, and turn the washer on, I don't need any faith at all. I *know* the washer is going to wash and rinse the clothes. I know when they're clean, I can put them in the dryer. After the prescribed number of minutes, my clothes will be dry. I don't have to wonder or worry. I just believe that my washer and dryer are going to work.

I have an automatic dishwasher that I trust implicitly. I put the dirty dishes in there, turn it on, and go sit down someplace and read my Bible without worrying a single bit. I don't pray each time for the dishwasher to work, and then keep opening the door to see if it is working. I just believe that it will fulfill its purpose.

I have tremendous faith in people too. I believe with my heart and soul that when I walk over to the wall and flip a little switch, light is going to illuminate the room I'm in. Even though I have never seen the man who owns the electric company, I have faith that electric power will be available when I need it.

I haven't seen the man who runs the water company either. However, I have faith that water will be available when I need it in the bathroom, the kitchen, or outside to water the lawn.

Look again at the examples I've given you. We all use electricity and water. In addition, we have faith in the grocer to give us food that is not spoiled or tainted. We have faith in the dairies to provide milk, cream, cheese, yogurt, and ice cream.

We have faith in thousands of things because we have used and depended on them over and over and over again. The chair you sit in, the refrigerator that preserves your food, the stove that cooks your food, and your home that keeps you warm (or cool) and protected. Everything you use in everyday life requires faith that it will function as you desire or need.

The same thing is true of faith in God. I've never seen Him, but then I haven't seen the electric plant manager either. I don't see the postmen that deliver our mail all over the world, but I have faith that when I put a stamp on that envelope, those unseen people will deliver it to the correct person. Think about all the people you have faith in and remember how you got that faith!

God is far more dependable than any individual or company

you'll ever find. Discover what His Word promises, then act on His Word. Faith can never grow until you step out and use it. You would not have driven a car if you hadn't tried the first time. You would still be washing clothes by beating them on a rock if you hadn't tried a washing machine.

You may not have had much faith the first time you tried to drive a car, but after a lot of practice, you learned, didn't you? You may have put a dent or two in your car before you learned, but you kept on trying until you succeeded!

The same thing is true of God. The more you try God, the more faith you will have, and the stronger your faith will become. Just because someone exercises their faith more often than you, don't get discouraged. Don't compare your faith to anyone else's faith. Just believe that you're going to keep trying God until your faith becomes as strong as theirs or stronger.

> God hath dealt to every man the measure of faith.
> (Romans 12:3 KJV)

God doesn't give one of us more faith than another. To each He gives *the* measure of faith, and it's what we do with that same-sized measure that makes the difference. Exercise your faith, and watch it grow. If you don't exercise it, it will diminish! That's God's principle.

Sow a little, get a little. Sow a lot, get a lot! He wants to make faith such a simple little gift. We often try to make it difficult because we're afraid to use it. I'd be afraid not to exercise faith, because Romans 14:23 says, "For whatsoever is not of faith is sin" (KJV).

God makes it so simple when He speaks to us. How do we possess the land that the Lord has given us, the land of faith, the land of health, the land of prosperity, and the land of happiness? Look how easy God makes it for us in Romans.

ANNIHILATE FEAR

> The word is nigh thee, even in thy mouth, and in thy heart: that is, the word of faith, which we preach; that if thou shalt confess with thy mouth the Lord Jesus, and shalt believe in thine heart that God hath raised him from the dead, thou shalt be saved. For with the heart man believeth unto righteousness; and with the mouth confession is made unto salvation. (Romans 10:8–10 KJV)

> With the mouth, confession is made *unto* salvation.
> With the mouth, confession is made *unto* healing.
> With the mouth, confession is made *unto* prosperity.

Develop the things that you *need* in your life by confessing them.

> Death and life are in the power of the tongue: and they that love it shall eat the fruit thereof. (Proverbs 18:21 KJV)

Depending on the words you choose to speak, you can have spiritual death or you can have life unspeakable and full of glory.

> You love him even though you have never seen him. Though you do not see him now, you trust him; and you rejoice with a glorious, inexpressible joy. (1 Peter 1:8 NLT)

We drove past a broken-down farmhouse and buildings somewhere in the State of Michigan. There was a large sign posted on the front fence. The property looked exactly as the sign it proclaimed, "Poverty Acres." You have what you say. And that's exactly what they had, poverty acres! If I had a farm, I would name it "Prosperity Paradise," or words similar to that, because I would speak it into a paradise that was prosperous.

> Thou art snared with the words of thy mouth, thou art taken with words of thy mouth. (Proverbs 6:2 KJV)

Then go to work like an ant (see Proverbs 6:3–12). Watch what you say. It's life or death. I prefer life. I choose life. I choose prosperity.

If you need prosperity, start confessing prosperity. How do you confess prosperity? Learn the "prosperity" Scriptures in the Bible! Begin confessing them daily to the walls of your house if you don't have anyone else to confess them to.

> Faith cometh by hearing, and hearing by the word of God. (Romans 10:17 KJV)

The more you hear the Word of God by confessing it with your own mouth, the more it will belong to you. Start going around your house quoting Scriptures you want to manifest in your life.

> But God shall supply all my need according to His riches in glory by Christ Jesus! (Philippians 4:19 KJV)

My God shall supply *all* my needs according to His riches in glory by Christ Jesus! Let me repeat that. My God shall supply *all* my needs according to His riches in glory by Christ Jesus! Glory to God, I don't have any needs because God is doing just what He said He would, He's supplying ALL my need.

As I was thinking about this book, thanking God for *the* measure of faith, I suddenly realized that God had already given me *all* the faith I would ever need. He has given me the *entire* measure of faith. He hasn't given me a tiny little portion; He has given me the whole *measure of faith*.

I don't have to ask for more, or wish for more, or pray for more. I have it! It was given to me when I was born again, and all I have to do is keep using it and stepping out into deeper and deeper spiritual water. I know that *the* measure, the all-in-all measure of faith is already mine.

    I possess it!
    I confess it!
    I have it!
    Faith is mine!
    Hallelujah!

Beloved, I wish above all things that thou mayest prosper and be in health, even as thy soul prospers.
(3 John 2 KJV)

    Start confessing right now: "I am prospering and in health because my soul is prospering! I am prospering and in health because my soul is prospering!" Keep saying that until it becomes a reality to you.

    Several years ago, Mom and Dad built their first office building. The day they moved in, they felt it was so big they would never be able to fill it up. It wasn't long before they realized they needed more space to handle the offices, mail, and shipping.

    One day, a lady gave them a check for $150 and said, "God told me to give this to you for your new building."

    Mom said, "You've got to be kidding. We're not going to build another building."

    The lady responded, "But God said you were."

    The next morning the telephone rang. It was the man who owned the property next door. The Hunter Ministry building was on a corner, so they could only expand one way—north. The property owner told Dad that he had a buyer for two-thirds of the property to the north, but he did not want the one-third next to us. Did Mom and Dad want it? After having received a check for

$150 the night before, they realized God had really gotten down to business in a hurry.

Dad asked how much they wanted for the property. The man responded with "$1.35 per foot or about $40,000."

Dad said, "Just a moment, please." He looked up and asked, "God, shall we buy it?"

The answer didn't take a second to come right back: "Yes!"

Dad told the man, "Yes!"

"When do you want to close?"

"Just a moment, please," Dad said. "God, when do we want to close?"

And God said, "As soon as possible."

"How do you want to pay for it, by cash, a loan with your bank, or a loan with us?"

Dad said, "Just a moment, please."

He prayed, and God said, "Cash!"

Dad said, "Cash!"

"How about a week from Wednesday. Is that all right?"

Dad said, "Just a moment, please."

He prayed again. God said, "Fine!"

Dad said, "Fine!" He hung up the telephone and looked at Mom. They both knew the funds in Hunter Ministries were exceptionally low. Even their personal bank account had never been so low. But, they knew that God had spoken. How did they know it? By faith!

In Mom's words, "We could have done one of two things. We could exercise our faith, or we could be overcome with doubts and fears wondering where the money was going to come from. We exercised our faith.

We went to church on Sunday and gave $100 as a regular tithe, and then $400 extra as a seed faith for the $40,000. I'll never forget how sincerely we laid hands on our Bible with the checks folded between Matthew 19:29 and Luke 6:38."

> "And anyone who gives up his home, brothers, sisters, father, mother, wife, children, or property, to follow me, shall receive a hundred times as much in return, and shall have eternal life." (Matthew 19:29 TLB)

> "For if you give, you will get! Your gift will return to you in full and overflowing measure, pressed down, shaken together to make room for more, and running over. Whatever measure you use to give—large or small—will be used to measure what is given back to you." (Luke 6:38 TLB)

Mom continued, "We *knew* it was done because we were doing our part in sowing the seed. We confessed God's Word about giving. We believed it in our hearts without a doubt and went off on a speaking trip. When we came back on Tuesday night before the closing on Wednesday morning, there was exactly $40,000 in the Hunter Ministries bank account!

More money had come in during that short period of time than had ever come in before during an equal period of time. We exercised our *faith*. We didn't pray and ask God to give us more faith. We simply exercised the measure of faith which He gave us at salvation. If it's prosperity you need, start confessing prosperity right now instead of confessing more bills than you can pay!"

My instruction to you today is, confess what God's Word says instead of what you think. I learned this from Mom and Dad. Now it's your turn to learn and practice.

God's Word is better than yours! Amen? Memorizing Scripture and quoting it aloud is the best way I know of to keep your faith increasing. Some of the easiest verses in the Bible to learn are in the first chapter of Psalms, which is loaded with promises.

> Blessed is the man that walketh not in the way of the counsel of the ungodly, nor standeth in the way of sinners, nor sitteth in the seat of the scornful. But his delight is in the law of the Lord, and in his law doth he meditate day and night. And he shall be like a tree planted by the rivers of water, that bringeth forth his fruit in his season; his leaf also shall not wither; and whatsoever he doeth shall prosper. (Psalm 1:1–3 KJV)

Memorize it and say it over and over again until it becomes a living part of you and you believe it in your heart. Then you can start saying:

"Thank You, Father, that I'm blessed because I don't walk in the counsel of the ungodly."

"Thank You, Father, that I'm blessed because I don't stand in the way of sinners."

"Thank You, Father, that I'm blessed because I don't sit in the seat of the scornful."

"Thank You, Father, that I'm blessed because I'm just like a tree planted by the rivers of water that bringeth forth his fruit in his season. Thank You, thank You, Father, that I'm planted right by the rivers of living water."

"Thank You, Father, that Your Word says that 'whatsoever' and that means anything that I do is going to prosper."

"Thank You, Father, that I have prosperity, because Your Word says that *everything, everything, everything* I do is going to prosper. *Everyone* I touch will prosper!"

Repeat those verses every day for thirty days, and you will begin to see the fruit of your words. They will begin to come to pass, because the words that you have spoken are not your words, they are God's words, and God cannot lie!

If healing were the thing I wanted most, I would memorize all the healing Scriptures. I would say them over and over again. I'd confess them until they became a reality in my life.

When you do this, you line up with what God says instead of what you say in the natural. You are building your faith. As you speak God's words, your faith grows. Suddenly, you will see your words manifest in your life.

> Bless the Lord, O my soul, and forget not all his benefits: Who forgiveth all thine iniquities, who healeth all thy diseases. (Psalm 103:2–3 KJV)

"Thank You, Lord, that You keep reminding me not to forget *all* your benefits. Thank You, Lord, that You have healed all my diseases. Thank You, Lord, that I don't have to suffer with them, because you *healed* every single one of them. I thank You, Lord, that it's done in the name of Jesus!"

A few more verses to build your faith:

> My son, attend to my words; incline thine ear unto my sayings. Let them not depart from thine eye. Keep them in the midst of thine heart. For they are life unto those that find them, and health to all their flesh. (Proverbs 4:20–22 KJV)

"Thank You, Lord. Because I pay attention to Your words, I listen to whatever You say. I love Your law and meditate in it day and night. I memorize Your Word and keep it in the midst of my heart. I have health to my flesh. *I have health to my flesh.* I have long life because Your Word says so."

> He sent His Word and healed them. (Psalm 107:20)

"Thank You, Lord, You sent Your Word in the flesh for the healing of the nations. Thank You and praise You, Lord, because You sent Your Word for my personal healing."

> He said, "If you will listen carefully to the voice of the Lord your God and do what is right in his sight, obeying his commands and keeping all his decrees, then I will not make you suffer any of the diseases I sent on the Egyptians; for I am the Lord who heals you." (Exodus 15:26 NLT)

My confession is: "Thank You, Lord, that I can listen to Your voice constantly, and I do that which is right in Your sight. I listen to Your commandments and keep Your statutes. Therefore, You will not put any diseases upon me because You are the Lord that heals me. Thank You, Lord, that I can depend on You. You are sitting right next to me telling me that You are the Lord that heals me. You mean me, not just somebody who lived during Bible times before I was born. Thank You, Lord, that these promises are mine *today*! In Jesus' precious name. Amen."

Start thanking Him!

> But he was wounded for our transgressions, he was bruised for our iniquities: the chastisement of our peace was upon Him; and with His stripes we are healed. (Isaiah 53:5 KJV)

"Thank You, Lord, that the lashings, the horrendous whipping You took in my place paid the price for my healing. Thank You that we operate by faith and not by sight. The things that are seen are temporal, but the things that are not seen are eternal. Thank You, Lord, that I am ruled by my spirit-man who believes what You say and not what my flesh says."

Your faith will develop the more you say and confess His words. Every time you repeat His words, it gives God another opportunity to answer. Each time He answers, your faith increases.

I had difficulty with that Scripture because I could accept the part about transgressions and sin being forgiven by the blood, but I had problems with the healing part.

Then I realized that I could not *see* my salvation, yet I *knew* it was there. I could not *see* the healing, yet it was there.

In the same way I believed in salvation, I would have to believe in healing that I could not see with my natural eyes. This was difficult to understand, but little by little, it became a reality.

We confess health daily. We confess prosperity daily. We confess happiness daily. We confess the Word of God daily. The more we confess the Word of God, the more each of these areas becomes a reality and a *living* part of our lives.

> But without faith it is impossible to please him: for he that cometh to God must believe that he is, and that he is a rewarder of them that diligently seek him. (Hebrews 11:6)

I want to please God more than anything. I want to do everything that I can possibly do on this earth to please God, therefore I'm certainly not going to risk displeasing Him when He says so plainly, "You can't please me if you don't exercise your faith!"

It isn't a question of simply having faith, because that has already been given to us. It is a question of exercising that faith.

Suddenly, it dawned on me one day that if I don't agree with the Word of God and speak it the way it is written, I am actually disagreeing with God. I am calling God and His Word a complete lie.

I certainly don't want to do that. Which is right: what *you* say or what *God* says?

DEVELOP YOUR FAITH

> Not one promise from God is empty of power, for nothing is impossible with God! (Luke 1:37 TPT)

Whether you believe His Word or not, it is not void of power. Speak His Word. Confess His Word. Read and repeat it until you see its power and it becomes a reality in your life.

A young boy named Jeff had a great influence in my parents' lives. His story is a perfect example of faith. He was five years old and lived outside of Louisville, Kentucky. He was born with cerebral palsy.

His precious parents were reading one of Mom and Dad's books that described God doing miracles in this modern day. They picked up a newspaper and discovered Mom and Dad were going to be speaking the next day in their area. They thought the meeting was a miracle service when it was actually a teaching service.

However, God doesn't care if a meeting is scheduled to be a healing or teaching service. When there is healing to be done, God does it any time and any place.

Mom and Dad saw this darling little boy whose body was so crippled from cerebral palsy. The Holy Spirit then took over the meeting, and man's plan for the evening was scrapped. Suddenly, God spoke to Mom, "Pray for Jeff right now. Right now!" She stepped down from the pulpit and walked over to Jeff's father who was holding him. She simply said, "God told me to pray for Jeff right now. May I have him for a few minutes?"

He said, "Yes."

Mom carried Jeff back onto the stage and sat down with him on one of the chairs. She likes to relax a child first, so she said, "Do you love Jesus?"

Jeff got a big smile on his face and replied, "Oh, yeah!"

Mom said, "Do you believe Jesus can heal you?"

Jeff continued to smile as he proclaimed, "Oh, He is going to heal me!" There was no doubt in his mind at all. This five-year-old boy simply believed Jesus was going to heal him that day.

While Mom held him in her loving arms, Dad laid his hands upon Jeff's head and they simply said, "Thank You, Lord. Thank You for an opportunity to show your great and mighty power. Father, as we envelop Jeff in our arms, may Your mighty power flow through him. Let Your healing power flow through this child's body in the name of Jesus!"

They continued for a few minutes saying, "Thank You, Lord Jesus! Thank You, Lord Jesus!"

Dad asked Jeff's parents if they would like to remove Jeff's braces. They immediately said, "Yes!" With Jeff sitting on a chair, they carefully removed the braces.

Dad looked a Jeff and then turned to look down the long aisle of the church. He then said, "Jeff, in the name of Jesus, *run!*"

Jeff got off that chair and stood looking down that aisle. He had never run in his life. He had never crawled because of the lack of motor coordination from the cerebral palsy. But he suddenly took off and ran—down the stairs, all the way to the back of that long aisle and back. They had never seen a child run that fast. His parents collapsed into their chairs in tears.

Mom stood in front of the pulpit and put her arms out to this precious child. When Jeff got about six feet from Mom, he made a flying leap into her arms and wrapped his arms and legs around her. He had never run in his life, yet when Jesus touched him, he just took off.

Mom looked at him and said, "Honey, who healed you?" She didn't want any credit for this miracle.

He looked back at her and said with a big smile, "*Jesus* healed me!"

When Mom and Dad said goodbye to these very grateful

and happy parents, Jeff's mom said, "You can keep those braces, because Jeff will never need them again. We are going out to buy him his first pair of regular shoes today."

Mom and Dad kept those braces in a glass cabinet as a constant reminder of the mighty power of God. When they talked to Jeff's parents a few weeks later, Jeff was doing great and had seen his pediatrician. The doctor said, "It's absolutely magnificent. This is fantastic!"

We praise God that when two or more are gathered together in His name, there He is right in the midst. He says you can ask for anything and He'll give it to you. God doesn't share His glory with anyone. All the glory goes to Him.

Jeff's sister took him to school the week after he was healed as her special "show and tell." What a witness! One year later, Mom and Dad saw Jeff again. He was doing great!

Why did Mom and Dad's faith grow so much with Jeff's healing? Every time you see a prayer answered, your faith grows. If they had not stepped out in faith, nothing would have happened. Jeff would not have been healed and their faith would not have been ignited.

If you want to increase your faith, pray more prayers. Somewhere along the line, you are going to step over into the realm of faith and action. Your faith will rise like a rocket.

Your faith can never grow to possess the entire *measure* of faith God gave you unless you exercise it. One of the greatest boosts to increase your faith is found in Hebrews.

> This is not the time to pull away and neglect meeting together, as some have formed the habit of doing, because we need each other! In fact, we should come together even more frequently, eager to encourage

and urge each other onward as we anticipate that day dawning. (Hebrews 10:25 TPT)

It is much easier for your faith to increase when you hear someone give their testimony of what God is doing in their life. When I hear testimonies, my spirit-man soars to new heights. We can all be built up in faith if we get together with other exciting Christians.

If you associate with people who are speaking faith, your faith will grow. If you hang around people speaking unbelief, your doubt will drown out your faith. It is essential to make contact and communicate with believers whose faith is at a high level.

This is why conventions and conferences are so helpful. Stay around believers who will boost your faith with their testimonies. Stay away from people who are filled with negativity and doubt. Confess the Word of God and build your faith. Try it for just thirty days and see what happens to you.

I am blessed because I am a child of God. I have the measure of faith God blessed me with. I don't have just a tiny little bit; I have the total measure of faith from God that I need to be what He has called me to be. I confess it. I possess it! I have it all! It is mine!

Review Psalm 1:3 again. Then repeat the following: "I have prosperity because the Word of God says that everything I do shall prosper. I am prospering! I have health because the Word of God says that my leaf shall not wither. God is the One who heals all my diseases. God's Word says that His Word is life and health to all who find them. I have been redeemed from the curse, and therefore I will not experience any of the diseases which were put upon the Egyptians. I have health because the Word of God says I am healed! I am walking by faith and not by sight. My body is lining up with the Word of God."

DEVELOP YOUR FAITH

For we walk by faith, not by sight. (2 Corinthians 5:7)

I confess it!
I possess it!
I have it!
It is mine!

Faith is my weapon against the enemy! I will not walk in fear again!

God gave me just enough faith for my assignment. I plan on using every bit of it to gain the victory against the enemy.

"Thank You, Jesus! My faith lies in You! I will never doubt or wonder if you can take care of me or my family. I depend on You! I will follow Your leading! I love You and will hold You close forever.

Thank You, Father!"

7

WHAT DOES LOVE HAVE TO DO WITH IT?

That question was the title of a popular song years ago. What is the answer? Love is the answer to everything. My God is pure unadulterated love which means:

GOD IS THE ANSWER TO EVERYTHING!

When you open your eyes in the morning, look to Him for what your day will bring. It doesn't matter if you wake up in a comfortable beautiful bed or on a street corner. God loves you and has placed you right where He wants you to fulfill your destiny and assist people around you to reach their destiny also.

You undoubtedly have experienced numerous challenges along your journey. You will handle many more before your work is over. You have faced and overcome fear from various directions and have come through with victory. You may even just call it survival, but at a basic level, God has brought you through whether you have given Him credit for your victory or not.

Once you accept Jesus as your Savior and receive the revelation of God as your Creator and Father, your eyes and heart can open wide to everything He has done for you since your birth. Look around and realize He has provided for you in love. If you have more than one outfit or one pair of shoes to wear, you have more than Jesus' disciples ever had. They also walked everywhere, while you drive or ride a bus or Uber.

With God as your Father, Jesus as your Brother, and the Holy Spirit as your Comforter and Guide, why live with fear in your back pocket? When fear tries to attack you, do you agree with the enemy's lies and pull fear out of that pocket to block your progress through your next challenge?

After reading this far in this book, you know you should immediately block any form of fear with faith in your Father God. He is your protection. He hasn't sent fear in any form to test you or stop you. However, He may allow the attack to see if you remember to pull out your weapons to fight the enemy.

If you haven't learned your lesson, you may have to repeat it again until you respond quickly and draw your weapon appropriately to ward off the lies of the devil.

The enemy tried to thwart Jesus' mission, His assignment. Look at what Jesus had to walk through and endure to give us salvation and open the doors to eternal life. He could have succumbed to fear so many times. Could you walk the walk knowing you would hang on a cruel cross, crucified for other people's sins?

Jesus was committed to His Father's plans. God gave Him what He needed to complete His thirty-three years on this earth. In return, God gave Jesus everyone who would believe in Him and follow Him. At this point in this book, I believe you believe in Him and desire to follow Him into history and heaven.

Jesus taught His disciples. God inspired several of those disciples to share His teachings with us through the Bible. God gave us the tools we need to fight the battle and win.

Do you remember the armor of God? It protects you every

minute of every day as long as you use it. No one else can wear this armor for you. No one can put it on you. You must put it on for yourself. Put it on every morning. You can even put it on before you open your eyes.

> Finally, be strong in the Lord and in his mighty power. Put on the full armor of God, so that you can take your stand against the devil's schemes. For our struggle is not against flesh and blood, but against the rulers, against the authorities, against the powers of this dark world and against the spiritual forces of evil in the heavenly realms.
>
> Therefore put on the full armor of God, so that when the day of evil comes, you may be able to stand your ground, and after you have done everything, to stand. Stand firm then, with the belt of truth buckled around your waist, with the breastplate of righteousness in place, and with your feet fitted with the readiness that comes from the gospel of peace. In addition to all this, take up the shield of faith, with which you can extinguish all the flaming arrows of the evil one. Take the helmet of salvation and the sword of the Spirit, which is the word of God.
>
> And pray in the Spirit on all occasions with all kinds of prayers and requests. With this in mind, be alert and always keep on praying for all the Lord's people. (Ephesians 6:10–18 NIV)

Put on the helmet of salvation and the breastplate of righteousness. Protect yourself with His truth. Walk in peace. Pick up the shield of faith and the sword of the Spirit. Open your mouth and praise Him! Exercise your faith. Allow the love of

God to flow through you. Pray without ceasing because the Holy Spirit will always help you with the words to say and the direction to walk today and every day thereafter.

What does love have to do with it? Say it this way: What does God (Love) have to do with it? He has everything to do with us, His children. He is our Source. He gives us life and breath. He protects us, He supplies what we need. He is the ultimate answer for all things and to all questions.

He loved us so much before any of us were even born, He provided a way to reconcile us back to right standing with Him. We can't be perfect enough to reach heaven on our own. In our own flesh, we can't do anything to even walk into His presence. However, He gave us Jesus to pay the ultimate price so we could live forever with them in heaven.

When we follow His instructions with obedience and trust, He is responsible to take care of us and supply us with what we need to complete His assignment. I don't believe He will ever send you or me on assignment without the necessary tools to be successful.

We may make our own elaborate plans without consulting Him. In that scenario, we are responsible for the details, not God. He may protect us from our own follies; however, success still depends on Him and our obedience to His instructions.

Do you want to live without fear? Stay within His love and protection. In other words, keep your shield of faith (in Him) held high. God may direct you to go into a situation which has the potential to bring on fear. However, if He has sent you, He has also equipped you. Remember that!

Maybe you have always gotten very nervous (which is a form of fear) about talking in front of people. The enemy has lied to you for years: "You aren't good enough. No one wants to hear what you have to say. They will just make fun of you. Don't open your mouth."

God designed your destiny before you were born. He wants you to teach (or preach) His Word. He has given you great wisdom and insight into His Word, which may be wasted if you don't accept His plans and step out with His courage to strengthen you.

Have you ever gotten a word or prophecy about ministering to others? Did you question those words or realize God was trying to get your attention? Listen for His voice, His instructions, His guidance.

Rebuke fear! Turn away from the negative! Read Scriptures on faith! Walk in His love and joy!

Jesus walked on the water. There are documented accounts of other people also walking on the water to fulfill their instructions from God. That day, Peter stepped out on the water at Jesus' command but then fell into disbelief and started sinking. Only when he fixed his eyes on Jesus and reached out for Jesus' hand did he safely walk with Jesus on the water to the safety of the fishing boat (see Matthew 14:25–33).

When you feel you are sinking, fix your eyes on Jesus. He will pick you up and empower you with what you need to keep on going. Every step will be that of Jesus carrying you to victory.

Where are you today? Do you feel God in your room? Maybe you are in a hospital bed. Can you feel Jesus' arms around you? Do you fear every medical person who enters your room? Instead, pray for every person who comes to your corner of that building. You don't know who God is sending to you who needs His love. Be open and sensitive to His voice.

Walk in His faith, His love.

You choose who you follow. Do you want to listen to the lies of the enemy that lead to fear? Or do you want to hear God's loving words that lead you to faith in everything He does or says?

ANNIHILATE FEAR

> But the fruit of the Spirit is love, joy, peace, longsuffering, kindness, goodness, faithfulness, gentleness, self-control. Against such there is no law. (Galatians 5:22–23)

Do you want to walk in the fruit of the Spirit? Imagine walking in His love, joy, peace, patience, kindness, goodness, faithfulness, gentleness, and self-control. Sounds like heaven, doesn't it?

We are to pattern our life after God, in His image. There is nothing to compare to the glorious feeling of God's love working through your voice, your hands, your love as you reach out to the lost, the sick, and the hurting people of the world. Jesus showed God to the people through His actions while on earth. We are to do the same.

> Jesus explained, "I am the Way, I am the Truth, and I am the Life. No one comes next to the Father except through union with me. To know me is to know my Father too. And from now on you will realize that you have seen him and experienced him." Philip spoke up, "Lord, show us the Father, and that will be all that we need!"
>
> Jesus replied, "Philip, I've been with you all this time and you still don't know who I am? How could you ask me to show you the Father, for anyone who has looked at me has seen the Father. Don't you believe that the Father is living in me and that I am living in the Father? Even my words are not my own but come from my Father, for he lives in me and performs his miracles of power through me. Believe that I live as one with my Father and that my Father lives as one with me—or at least, believe because of the mighty miracles I have done." (John 14:6–11 TPT)

WHAT DOES LOVE HAVE TO DO WITH IT?

Every morning, put on the armor of God, add the fruit of the Spirit, and step out in total faith with Him working through you.

If anything negative tries to enter, rebuke it. This includes the works of the flesh:

> Now the works of the flesh are evident, which are: adultery, fornication, uncleanness, lewdness, idolatry, sorcery, hatred, contentions, jealousies, outbursts of wrath, selfish ambitions, dissensions, heresies, envy, murders, drunkenness, revelries, and the like; of which I tell you beforehand, just as I also told you in time past, that those who practice such things will not inherit the kingdom of God. (Galatians 4:19–21)

If you recognize the works of the enemy or his lies, act immediately to remove them from your life! Such works of the flesh will open the door to fear. Don't welcome fear back into your life. It is your choice and only your choice.

Don't accept the negative words spewed out of the enemy's mouth. Rebuke him and run to God.

Walk in His love. Faith in Him multiplies the love shared between you and your Father. Love grows when you have faith in a person such as your child, parent, or spouse.

As your faith in a person increases, love develops and grows also. The same thing happens as your relationship with God gets closer and closer.

Your love for His Word will also grow. Speak His Word. Listen for His voice.

Love and faith will annihilate fear in every area of your life.

As an apostle, I now commission and send you out to free those paralyzed by fear, trapped in the lies of the enemy. Set

ANNIHILATE FEAR

yourself free and then set others free also. Bring freedom to the children of God.
    CHOOSE LOVE!
    CHOOSE FAITH!
    ANNHILATE FEAR!

AFTERWORD

Earlier in this book, I challenged you to write down your thoughts or understanding of fear, faith, and love and their relationship with each other.

I now ask you to look over what you wrote. Has your understanding changed? Do you know what to do if fear rears its ugly head in your situation?

On the following pages you will find Scriptures and prayers written just for you so you can continue to build your faith and annihilate fear.

Thank you for reading this book. Please share what you learned with others. Stay in love, stay in freedom.

Until next time, blessings, blessings and more blessings.

Joan

SCRIPTURES

HEALTHY FEAR / AWE / REVERENCE FOR GOD

The fear of the Lord is the beginning of wisdom; a good understanding have all those who do His commandments. His praise endures forever. (Psalm 111:10)

Blessed is every one who fears the Lord, who walks in His ways. (Psalm 128:1 TPT)

Behold, thus shall the man be blessed Who fears the Lord. (Psalm 128:4)

He will fulfill the desire of those who fear Him; He also will hear their cry and save them. (Psalm 145:19)

The Lord takes pleasure in those who fear Him, in those who hope in His mercy. (Psalm 147:11)

ANNIHILATE FEAR

The fear of the Lord is the beginning of knowledge, but fools despise wisdom and instruction. (Proverbs 1:7)

"Fear not, little flock, for it is your Father's good pleasure to give you the kingdom." (Luke 12:32 ESV)

Oh, how great is Your goodness, which You have laid up for those who fear You, which You have prepared for those who trust in You in the presence of the sons of men! (Psalm 31:19)

Behold, the eye of the Lord is on those who fear Him, on those who hope in His mercy. (Psalm 33:18)

The angel of the Lord encamps around those who fear Him [with awe-inspired reverence and worship Him with obedience], and He rescues [each of] them. (Psalm 34:7 AMP)

But to man He said, "Behold, the reverential and worshipful fear of the Lord—that is wisdom; And to depart from evil is understanding." (Job 28:28 AMP)

SCRIPTURES

GOD'S PROTECTION

Fear not, for I am with you; be not dismayed, for I am your God. I will strengthen you, yes, I will help you, I will uphold you with My righteous right hand. (Isaiah 41:10)

But now, thus says the Lord, who created you, O Jacob, and He who formed you, O Israel: "Fear not, for I have redeemed you; I have called you by your name; You are Mine. (Isaiah 43:1)

Fear not, for I am with you; be not dismayed, for I am your God; I will strengthen you, I will help you, I will uphold you with my righteous right hand. (Isaiah 41:10 ESV)

Have I not commanded you? Be strong and courageous. Do not be frightened, and do not be dismayed, for the Lord your God is with you wherever you go. (Joshua 1:9 ESV)

For I, the Lord your God, hold your right hand; it is I who say to you, "Fear not, I am the one who helps you." (Isaiah 41:13 ESV)

The Lord is on my side; I will not fear. What can man do to me? (Psalm 118:6 ESV)

The fear of man lays a snare, but whoever trusts in the Lord is safe. (Proverbs 29:25 ESV)

ANNIHILATE FEAR

The Lord is my light and my salvation; whom shall I fear? The Lord is the stronghold of my life; of whom shall I be afraid? (Psalm 27:1 ESV)

Be strong and courageous. Do not fear or be in dread of them, for it is the Lord your God who goes with you. He will not leave you or forsake you. (Deuteronomy 31:6 ESV)

I sought the Lord, and he answered me and delivered me from all my fears. (Psalm 34:4 ESV)

It is the Lord who goes before you. He will be with you; he will not leave you or forsake you. Do not fear or be dismayed. (Deuteronomy 31:8 ESV)

For you did not receive the spirit of slavery to fall back into fear, but you have received the Spirit of adoption as sons, by whom we cry, "Abba! Father!" (Romans 8:15 ESV)

So we can confidently say, "The Lord is my helper; I will not fear; what can man do to me?" (Hebrews 13:6 ESV)

But even if you should suffer for righteousness' sake, you will be blessed. Have no fear of them, nor be troubled. (1 Peter 3:14 ESV)

SCRIPTURES

Though an army may encamp against me, My heart shall not fear; though war may rise against me, in this I will be confident. (Psalm 27:3)

I sought the Lord, and He heard me, and delivered me from all my fears. (Psalm 34:4)

"You must not fear them, for the Lord your God Himself fights for you." (Deuteronomy 3:22)

FAITH

When I am afraid, I put my trust in you.
(Psalm 56:3 ESV)

Even though I walk through the valley of the shadow of death, I will fear no evil, for you are with me; your rod and your staff, they comfort me. (Psalm 23:4 ESV)

Casting all your anxieties on him, because he cares for you. (1 Peter 5:7 ESV)

Do not be anxious about anything, but in everything by prayer and supplication with thanksgiving let your requests be made known to God. And the peace of God, which surpasses all understanding, will guard your hearts and your minds in Christ Jesus. (Philippians 4:6–7 ESV)

Let not your hearts be troubled. Believe in God; believe also in me. (John 14:1 ESV)

But Jesus on hearing this answered him, "Do not fear; only believe, and she will be well." (Luke 8:50 ESV)

But when they saw him walking on the sea they thought it was a ghost, and cried out, for they all saw him and were terrified. But immediately he spoke to them and said, "Take heart; it is I. Do not be afraid." (Mark 6:49–50 ESV)

SCRIPTURES

"Look, the Lord your God has set the land before you; go up and possess it, as the Lord God of your fathers has spoken to you; do not fear or be discouraged." (Deuteronomy 1:21)

God, you're such a safe and powerful place to find refuge! You're a proven help in time of trouble—more than enough and always available whenever I need you. So we will never fear even if every structure of support were to crumble away. We will not fear even when the earth quakes and shakes, moving mountains and casting them into the sea. For the raging roar of stormy winds and crashing waves cannot erode our faith in you. (Psalm 46:1–2 TPT)

"Behold the proud, His soul is not upright in him; but the just shall live by his faith. (Habakkuk 2:4)

Just then Jesus turned around and looked at her and said, "My daughter, be encouraged. Your faith has healed you." And instantly she was healed! (Matthew 9:22 TPT)

Then Jesus put his hands over their eyes and said, "You will have what your faith expects!" (Matthew 9:29 TPT)

And tell John that the blessing of heaven comes upon those who never lose their faith in me—no matter what happens!" (Matthew 11:6 TPT)

ANNIHILATE FEAR

Then Jesus said to the healed man lying at his feet, "Arise and go. It was your faith that brought you salvation and healing." (Luke 17:19 TPT)

But all that is recorded here is so that you will fully believe that Jesus is the Anointed One, the Son of God, and that through your faith in him you will experience eternal life by the power of his name! (John 20:31 TPT)

Everything you pray for with the fullness of faith you will receive!" (Matthew 21:22 TPT)

Then Jesus said to the woman, "Your faith in me has given you life. Now you may leave and walk in the ways of peace." (Luke 7:50 TPT)

For because of our faith, he has brought us into this place of highest privilege where we now stand, and we confidently and joyfully look forward to actually becoming all that God has had in mind for us to be. (Romans 5:2 TLB)

SCRIPTURES

GOD'S FAITHFULNESS

I will sing of the mercies of the Lord forever; with my mouth will I make known Your faithfulness to all generations. (Psalm 89:1)

For I have said, "Mercy shall be built up forever; Your faithfulness You shall establish in the very heavens." (Psalm 89:2)

And the heavens will praise Your wonders, O Lord; Your faithfulness also in the assembly of the saints. (Psalm 89:5)

O Lord God of hosts, who is mighty like You, O Lord? Your faithfulness also surrounds You. (Psalm 89:8)

Then the Lord said to him, "Peace be with you; do not fear, you shall not die." (Judges 6:23)

LOVE

There is no fear in love, but perfect love casts out fear. For fear has to do with punishment, and whoever fears has not been perfected in love. (1 John 4:18 ESV)

For God gave us a spirit not of fear but of power and love and self-control. (2 Timothy 1:7 ESV)

Are not two sparrows sold for a penny? And not one of them will fall to the ground apart from your Father. But even the hairs of your head are all numbered. Fear not, therefore; you are of more value than many sparrows. (Matthew 10:29–31 ESV)

In God, whose word I praise, in God I trust; I shall not be afraid. What can flesh do to me? (Psalm 56:4 ESV)

As a father shows compassion to his children, so the Lord shows compassion to those who fear him. (Psalm 103:13 ESV)

There's a private place reserved for the lovers of God, where they sit near him and receive the revelation-secrets of his promises. (Psalm 25:14 TPT)

He satisfies all who love and trust him, and he keeps every promise he makes. (Psalm 111:5 TPT)

SCRIPTURES

The faithful love of the Lord never ends! His mercies never cease. Great is his faithfulness; his mercies begin afresh each morning. (Lamentations 3:22–24 NLT)

Your love is so extravagant it reaches to the heavens, Your faithfulness so astonishing it stretches to the sky! (Psalm 57:10 TPT)

But Lord, your nurturing love is tender and gentle. You are slow to get angry yet so swift to show your faithful love. You are full of abounding grace and truth. (Psalm 86:15 TPT)

GOD'S PROMISE TO SAVE YOUR FAMILY

Fear not, for I am with you; I will bring your descendants from the east, and gather you from the west. (Isaiah 43:5)

"Therefore know that the Lord your God, He is God, the faithful God who keeps covenant and mercy for a thousand generations with those who love Him and keep His commandments." (Deuteronomy 7:9)

Oh, that they had such a heart in them that they would fear Me and always keep all My commandments, that it might be well with them and with their children forever! (Deuteronomy 5:29)

For the Lord is always good and ready to receive you. He's so loving that it will amaze you— so kind that it will astound you! And he is famous for his faithfulness toward all. Everyone knows our God can be trusted, for he keeps his promises to every generation! (Psalm 100:5 TPT)

But Lord, your endless love stretches from one eternity to the other, unbroken and unrelenting toward those who fear you and those who bow facedown in awe before you. Your faithfulness to keep every gracious promise you've made passes from parents, to children, to grandchildren, and beyond. (Psalm 103:17 TPT)

SCRIPTURES

Your faithfulness flows from one generation to the next; all that you created sits firmly in place to testify of you. (Psalm 119:90 TPT)

REBUKE THE ENEMY

"And I will rebuke the devourer for your sakes, So that he will not destroy the fruit of your ground, Nor shall the vine fail to bear fruit for you in the field," says the Lord of hosts. (Malachi 3:11)

And Jesus rebuked the demon, and it came out of him; and the child was cured from that very hour. (Matthew 17:18)

But Jesus rebuked him, saying, "Be quiet, and come out of him!" (Mark 1:25)

When Jesus saw that the people came running together, He rebuked the unclean spirit, saying to it, "Deaf and dumb spirit, I command you, come out of him and enter him no more!" (Mark 9:25)

But Jesus rebuked him, saying, "Be quiet, and come out of him!" And when the demon had thrown him in their midst, it came out of him and did not hurt him. (Luke 4:35)

SCRIPTURES

BELIEVERS CAN USE THE NAME OF JESUS

When the seventy-two disciples returned, they joyfully reported to him, "Lord, even the demons obey us when we use your name!" (Luke 10:17 TLB)

"Through faith in the name of Jesus, this man was healed—and you know how crippled he was before. Faith in Jesus name has healed him before your very eyes. (Acts 3:16)

PRAYERS

This section provides powerful prayers for you to declare. Say the prayers provided on the following pages, and then continue to talk with the Lord. We've provided lines for you to write out your own prayers of faith. God's promises are given freely to His children. To be assured of His comfort, guidance, and provisions, you need to be saved. Salvation is given freely by your confession of faith in Jesus and welcoming Him to live in your heart. Begin with this prayer of salvation. God bless you!

SALVATION

Pray: Father, I know I have made mistakes, which are sin in Your eyes. Please forgive me for ignoring You and doing things that have kept me away from Your perfect will for my life. I turn from that life and rebuke the enemy's lies. I accept Jesus into my heart and the Holy Spirit as my Guide from this day forward. Thank You, Father. In Jesus' name. Amen.

TRAUMA

In Jesus' name, I command all the trauma stored in the cells of this body to go and not return. I also command the spirit of fear to leave. I command life and health in the tissues of this body to be restored and all hopelessness to leave. In Jesus' name. Amen.

FEAR OF DYING

I command the spirits of untimely death, suicide, and fear to leave in Jesus' name. I will live and not die, and declare the works of the Lord (Psalm 118:17). I will find new life and joy in Jesus Christ. When I have completed God's assignment for my life, I know without a shadow of a doubt that I will not die, but live for eternity with God in heaven. In Jesus' name. Amen.

FEAR OF ABUSE

Thank You, Lord Jesus, for healing me from all the physical, spiritual, and emotional abuse that I have experienced. I now command the spirit of fear of further abuse to be gone forever as well as all the lies of the enemy that I deserve to be abused. I know I can look ahead to a positive future with good relationships because You are with me. In Jesus' name. Amen.

PRAYERS

FEAR OF ABANDONMENT

I thank You, Father God, that You are always with me and watching over me, and that You will never forsake me. I am always comforted by Your love. I command the orphan spirit to leave me and not return. In Jesus' name. Amen.

FEAR OF LACK

Thank You, Father, for taking care of my needs and the needs of my family (Matthew 6:31–33). I know You will supply all our needs. I command that fear of lack to go, and I decree that You are my supply and my ever-present help in time of need. I will fear no evil. I command the spirit of poverty and the poverty mindset to go. I will always have food, water, and a safe place to lay my head. In Jesus' name. Amen.

FEAR OF INADEQUACY

Father, I thank You that I will no longer be paralyzed by a sense of my own limitations. God, you made me and You gave me all the abilities I need to complete Your plan for my life. I command that sense of inadequacy and inferiority to leave, and I embrace Your wisdom and power, knowing You are more than able to take care of me, no matter what I go through. In Jesus' name. Amen.

FEAR OF REJECTION

Thank You, Jesus, for healing my heart and spirit from all the experiences of rejection I have endured. I am happy and blessed because no matter who attacks me, You hold me close (Psalm 27:10). You were rejected in a far worse manner than I, and I know You will protect me from evil people. In Jesus' name. Amen.

FEAR OF FAILURE

Lord Jesus, thank You that You are releasing me now from the fear of failure that has kept me from fulfilling my God given purposes on earth. I trust You to give me the courage to try new things and that they will succeed because You are actively helping me. I cut off any word curses that have been spoken over me in all these areas and more. In Jesus' name. Amen.

FEAR OF LOVED ONES GOING TO HELL

Father, I pray for all my loved ones (name them). I don't know their status with You, but I am concerned that they may end up in hell instead of with You in heaven. Lead and guide them, Father, on the path You have planned for them. Please have someone come across their path who they will listen to, so they will get saved. In Jesus' name. Amen.

FEAR OF GENERATIONAL CURSES/DISEASES

Father, You have told us we can rebuke generational curses and diseases. Right now, I rebuke all curses and diseases that have come down my generational bloodline. They cannot stay in this body, in Jesus' name. I refuse any attack of the enemy in this area. He does not have permission to enter this body or drag generational problems into me or my family's lives. In Jesus' name. Amen.

FEAR OF DISEASE

Jesus, I need Your peace and love in my life. Please alert me to any spirit of disease that tries to divert or distract what You have planned for my life. I want to stay focused on You and where You lead me. In Jesus' name. Amen.

FEAR OF PHOBIAS

Father, there are many people who have developed unrealistic paralyzing fear of many things: people, heights, close spaces, travel, insects, and even leaving their house. I rebuke this spirit of fear in Jesus' name. I speak freedom and peace to this person to continue their journey you have planned for them. In Jesus' name. Amen.

ANNIHILATE FEAR

FEAR OF SPEAKING/SHARING TESTIMONY

Father, sharing salvation with others is part of the Great Commission given to all of Your children. The enemy comes along and plants fear of speaking to others or sharing a testimony with another person. I know that this communication is a key to bringing a nonbeliever to salvation by sharing the gospel. It also encourages another person to have faith in Your promises. I rebuke this fear in Jesus' name. I speak total freedom over this person, freedom to speak whenever You want them to speak to someone, whether an individual or a crowd. Give them the words to speak, in Jesus' name. Amen.

FEAR OF MINISTRY FOR HEALING

Father, You have instructed us to lay hands on the sick and see them healed. I rebuke any fear of ministering to others or to oneself. You don't tell us to do something without equipping us with the tools to complete our assignment. Thank You, Father, for the confidence and wisdom to minister to others. In Jesus' name. Amen.

ANNIHILATE FEAR

FEAR OF HOSPITALS/DOCTORS

Father, You have given special gifts to each of Your children to fulfill Your purpose for them. I rebuke any fear of hospitals or doctors who are doing Your work among the sick people. Give the medical people great wisdom and understanding to minister to those afflicted with disease or injury. Work through their hands and heart to continue Your work. In Jesus' name. Amen.

PRAYERS

FEAR OF PEOPLE/CONTROL/CO-DEPENDENCY

Father, I have allowed other people to control me—how I think, react, and live. I rebuke that spirit of control and co-dependency in Jesus' name. Father, please give me wisdom, confidence, freedom, and peace that I can manage my life and not react negatively to this person. I rebuke and bind the enemy off their life and mind also. Let them live in peace without the need to subject other people to their demands and threats. In Jesus' name. Amen.

FEAR OF POLITICAL UNREST/CONTROVERSY

Father, upheaval, riots, controversy, and violence are not from you. They are tools of the enemy. I rebuke the spirits of violence, fault finding, and anger in Jesus' name. I speak peace, contentment, love, and reconciliation over these people in Jesus' name. Amen.

SPIRIT OF FEAR/WORRY/ANXIETY/MENTAL ILLNESS

Father, some people are wrapped up in their own fears because they witness others who are plagued with worry and anxiety. Maybe a friend or family member has been diagnosed with mental illness. Father, please fill these people with Your love and peace. Let them know You will not leave them or forsake them—that You are the answer to their issues. Guide someone to each of them, Father, to share Your love and comfort. In Jesus' name. Amen.

ANNIHILATE FEAR

FEAR OF WEATHER, STORMS, DISASTERS

Father, we all like beautiful weather, but we know the rain has to fall to water the earth and all of Your creation. Storms are inevitable, and occasionally humanity faces disasters. People get scared and lose control of wisdom to survive. I rebuke that fear in Jesus' name. Show them, Father, that You are always there to help them get to safety. Protect the innocent, Father. I speak Your wisdom over each one facing a storm, whether mental, physical, or weather related. I speak peace. In Jesus' name. Amen.

PRAYERS

FEAR OF MISSING HEAVEN

Jesus, I believe in You. I know You willingly gave Your life to save those who believe in You. Jesus, I do believe in You and want You to live within me forever. I don't want to miss heaven because of doing something wrong. Please lead and guide me from this day onward. In Your blessed name I pray. Amen.

THANKFULNESS, APPRECIATION, AND LOVE

Father, thank You for salvation, reconciliation with You, and a path to eternal life in heaven with You. Jesus paid the price for my salvation, and I will be forever thankful for His sacrifice. There are not enough words to express my appreciation for Your choosing to allow me to live in this world. I love You, I love Jesus, and I love the Holy Spirit. I look forward to each day in Your world and to an eternity with You in heaven. Thank You, Father. I ask this in Jesus' name. Amen.

ACKNOWLEDGEMENTS

A special thanks to Naida Johnson for her valuable input and work editing this book. Also thanks to Kelley, my husband, for his incredible input, along with proofreading the book and verifying the Scriptures. You both were such a blessing to this project!

ABOUT THE AUTHOR

Joan's genuine approach and candid delivery enables her to connect intimately with people from all walks of life. Her focus is to train and equip believers to take the healing power of God beyond the 4 walls of the church and into the 4 corners of the earth!

At the young age of 12, Joan dedicated her heart to the Lord and has faithfully served him from that day to this. She exhibits a sincere desire to see the body of Christ set free in their body, mind, soul, spirit, and finances. Joan is a compassionate minister, dynamic teacher, an accomplished author, and an anointed healing evangelist.

Joan has ministered in countries all over the world and has been on numerous television and radio appearances. She hosts a powerful and exciting show of her own called *Miracles Happen!* She has authored more than 18 books and has recorded teachings that will encourage you and teach you how to pray for the sick and see them recover. Books and teachings are available to order through joanhunter.org and joanhunter.ca. Some resources are available as digital downloads through Amazon.com and iTunes.

Joan Hunter and her husband, Kelley, live northwest of Houston, Texas. Together, they have 4 daughters, 4 sons, 3 sons-in-law and 7 grandchildren. Joan is the daughter of the Happy Hunters, Charles and Frances Hunter.

Connect with Joan at JoanHunter.com or JoanHunter.ca.